EDWARD LUCE

THE RETREAT OF WESTERN LIBERALISM

Little, Brown

LITTLE, BROWN

First published in Great Britain in 2017 by Little, Brown

1 3 5 7 9 10 8 6 4 2

Copyright © Edward Luce 2017

The moral right of the author has been asserted.

Extract from 'Annus Mirabilis' on page 188 taken from *The Collected Poems* by Philip Larkin, published by Faber and Faber Ltd. © Estate of Philip Larkin.

A CIP catalogue record for this book
is available from the British Library.

Hardback ISBN 978-1-4087-1041-8
C-format ISBN 978-1-4087-1040-1

Typeset in Goudy by M Rules
Printed and bound in Great Britain by
Clays Ltd, St Ives plc

Papers used by Little, Brown are from well-managed forests
and other responsible sources.

Little, Brown
An imprint of
Little, Brown Book Group
Carmelite House
50 Victoria Embankment
London EC4Y 0DZ

An Hachette UK Company
www.hachette.co.uk

www.littlebrown.co.uk

THE

RETREAT

OF

WESTERN

LIBERALISM

Paris   11.08.17

Dear Papa de Edú,

From the grateful recipients
of his many articles that
you have sent us
over the years.

Edward & Inés

CONTENTS

Preface   1

1 Fusion   17

2 Reaction   75

3 Fallout   143

4 Half Life   185

Notes   205

Acknowledgements   219

Index   223

PREFACE

We learn from history that we do not learn from history.

FRIEDRICH HEGEL

A gaggle of students are driving at high speed to Berlin. 'Bliss was it in that dawn to be alive, / But to be young was very heaven,' wrote Wordsworth about the French Revolution. The poet's sentiments captured our mood. The year was 1989. Having grown up under the Cold War's nuclear shadow, the temptation to catch a glimpse of its physical demise was irresistible. Being students, we did not inform anyone of our absence. The instant we heard East Germany had opened Checkpoint Charlie, uniting Berlin, we were on our way. Four hours later we had boarded a ferry from Dover to Zeebrugge. Within eighteen hours we too – three boys and two girls – were chipping at that wall alongside tens of thousands of others, young and old, German and foreign. With chisels and pickaxes we made our tiny contributions to this orgy of historic vandalism. Friendships were forged with people whom we had never met, nor would again. One group of West Berliners hugged us and shared their bottle of champagne. Could there have been a more fitting way to toast the new era than with champagne from strangers? Two days later we returned to England, chronically hungover, astonished to have avoided any speeding tickets, carrying a small chunk of the wall apiece. I have since mislaid my souvenir. But my tutor, who had noted my absence, was mollified by my excuse. 'I suppose it's better than the alternatives,' he said when I showed him my bit of the wall. 'Did you have fun?'

We were infected with optimism. As a student of Philosophy, Politics and Economics at Oxford University, I imagined that I possessed the key to the historic significance of the moment. PPE's detractors called it a Pretty Poor Education. They may have had a point. But in that moment, all the late-night essay crises seemed to come together. A less derogatory phrase for PPE is Modern Greats, in reference to Oxford's venerable Greats degree in classics. In content, there is little comparison: Sophocles' tragedies bear scant relation to the desiccated logic of Oxford economics. But they share a conceit about the primacy of Western thought. On this, if little else, there is no quarrel between the ancients and the moderns. We called it progress, or rather Progress – belief in which is the closest thing the modern West has to a religion. In 1989 its schism was healed. By unifying its booming western wing with the shrivelled post-Stalinist eastern one, there was no longer any quarrel between the present and the present.

Shortly before the Berlin Wall fell, Francis Fukuyama published his famous essay, 'The End of History?'. 'What we may be witnessing is not just the end of the Cold War . . . but the end of history as such: that is, the end point of mankind's ideological evolution and the universalisation of Western liberal democracy as the final form of human government,' he wrote.[1] Though I did not subscribe to Fukuyama's view of the ideal society I shared his relief. A monumental roadblock had been cleared from our future. No longer would nuclear-armed ideological camps face each other across the twentieth-century bloodlands of central Europe. That riven continent, from which Britain no longer stood aloof, would unify. Democracies would take the place of the Warsaw Pact, whose regimes were falling like dominoes to peaceful demonstrators. It was not just autocracy that was dying but nationalism. Borders were opening up. Global horizons beckoned. A unipolar world was dawning. At a stroke, and without a shot being fired, our generation was staging the funeral rites for the twin scourges of Western modernity, communism and fascism. As the historian Eric Hobsbawm was to write, the short and genocidal twentieth century, which began with the Russian revolution in 1917, came to an end in 1989.[2] Though still alive, history was smiling. The human species had proved it could learn from its mistakes. It was a good year to turn twenty-one.

Nearly three decades later, in the aftermath of Donald Trump's 2016 election victory, I found myself in Moscow. I had been invited to attend a conference on the 'polycentric world order', which is Russian for 'post-American world'. The conference was hosted by the Primakov Institute, named after the man who had been Russia's foreign minister and prime minister during the 1990s. Yevgeny Primakov was displaced as prime minister in 1999 by Vladimir Putin. While my friends and I had danced on the rubble of the Berlin Wall, a brooding Putin had watched his world crumbling from 130 miles away, at his KGB office in Dresden, a city in what was still East Germany. Later he would describe the dissolution of the Soviet Union as the 'greatest geopolitical tragedy of the twentieth century'. It was Primakov who championed the term multipolarity in what at the time seemed like a vain bid to dampen America's oceanic post-Cold War triumphalism. Putin picked up the concept and made it his own. As the world's one indispensable power, Americans never warmed to the idea of multipolarity. Such was Washington's self-confidence that it even came to disdain the word multilateralism. As Madeleine Albright, the US Secretary of State in the late 1990s, put it, 'It has too many syllables and ends with an "ism".'

Now here I was in Moscow at an event attended by the likes of Alexander Bortnikov, head of the FSB (successor to the KGB), and Vladimir Putin himself. Though unsmiling, it was Russia's turn to celebrate. The institute had sent me its invitation several months earlier and I had promptly forgotten about it. On 9 November, the morning after the US presidential election, as I tried to make sense of the dawning new reality I recalled that invitation. By eerie coincidence, it was twenty-seven years to the day since the fall of the Berlin Wall. The worm had turned. America had just elected a president who was a big fan of walls and a big admirer of Vladimir Putin. While Putin was surveying his wrecked world in 1989, and we were racing down the *Autobahn*, Donald Trump was launching a board game. It was called Trump: The Game. With its fake paper money and property-based rules, it bore an uncanny resemblance to Monopoly – except that the number six on the dice was replaced with the letter T. Unsurprisingly, it was a flop. There is no record that Trump said anything positive or negative about the fall of the Berlin Wall. At any rate, all that seemed a long time ago. America had just elected a man who admired the way politics was done in Russia. His campaign had even profited from Moscow's assistance. Would the Russians kindly agree to my belated acceptance? They would indeed.

What followed was a crash course in how to see the world very differently. Still a student of history, though I hope by now a more sceptical one, I was struck by how often our Russian hosts referred admiringly to the Congress of Vienna. That was the 1814–15 conference that sealed the end of the Napoleonic Wars and launched almost a century of stability, which held until the outbreak of the First World War. The new order was underwritten by the Quadruple Alliance of Great Britain, Austria, Prussia and, most importantly, Russia. Trump's victory had opened up the prospect that Russia could return to its historic role as a great power in a polycentric world – one in which each happily forswore doing anything to undermine the internal legitimacy of any other. No more talk of the inevitability of democracy, or the US-led global order. That was what Putin craved. As for Crimea, which Putin annexed in 2014, inviting a spider's web of US-led sanctions, its absorption back into the motherland was now an irreversible fact. Crimea was only returning to the status it had before 1954, when Moscow, in a fit of administrative generosity, had transferred it to the then Soviet republic of Ukraine. John Kerry, the US Secretary of State under Obama, had condemned Russia's annexation of Crimea from the now-independent Ukraine as a violation of history: 'You just don't in the twenty-first century behave in nineteenth-century fashion by invading another country on [a] completely trumped-up pretext,' he said. But that is how the world often works. The US had done that to Iraq in the twenty-first century. In Moscow's view, history is back and nothing is inevitable, least of all liberal democracy. Others, in Beijing, Ankara, Cairo, Caracas, and even Budapest, share Russia's hostility to Western notions of progress, as do growing numbers of apostates in the West. Are they wrong?

This book is my attempt to answer that question. Let me declare now that nothing is pre-ordained. To a person whose life has coincided with the rise of democracy, the spread of market economics and signs that the world had finally subscribed to the Universal Declaration of Human Rights (even if much of it is paid only in lip service – hypocrisy, as they say, being the compliment vice pays to virtue), merely to pose the question is troubling enough. Wasn't that debate settled a long time ago? Isn't the march of human freedom unstoppable? Doesn't the whole world crave to be Western? We can no longer have any confidence in that. It was remarkably arrogant to believe the rest of the world would passively adopt our script. Those who still believe in the inevitable triumph of the Western model might ask themselves whether it is faith, rather than facts, that fuels their worldview. We must cast a sceptical eye on what we have learned never to question. Our sanity may be tested in the process.

At stake is a quasi-religious reading of Western history that stretches back to the Magna Carta, whose octocentennial was celebrated at Runnymede in 2015. By limiting the power of the king, the Magna Carta set a precedent for what would later be known as 'no taxation without representation'. This short medieval document was lost to the mists for several hundred years – Shakespeare did not even mention it in his play *King John*. Yet since the seventeenth century, when the Magna Carta was dusted off by opponents of Stuart tyranny in England, then made its way to America's thirteen colonies, it has morphed into the founding myth of Western liberalism. As Dan Jones, an historian of the Magna Carta, describes it, the year 1215 is today seen as the 'year zero' of Western liberalism.[3] It was cited as an inspiration by the Founding Fathers, by anti-colonial movements around the world, and is now finally celebrated in Britain itself. When the Universal Declaration of Human Rights was issued after the Second World War, Eleanor Roosevelt said that it 'may well become the international Magna Carta for all men everywhere'. That this covenant between John and his rebellious nobles lasted for only two months, awarded fixed privileges to the aristocracy and limited the rights of women and Jews, should give us some pause. Rather than a springboard to liberty, the Magna Carta was a messy expediency between a temporarily weakened king and his restive nobles. It quickly expired. That it is today so prized – a copy sits next to the Declaration of Independence in the US National Archives – is a measure of our amnesia. If the intellectual basis of Western liberalism is scepticism, we should learn to live up to its meaning.

We should be particularly wary of the siren song of history. George Santayana famously said, 'Those who cannot remember the past are condemned to repeat it'. The idea of history as a separate force with a mind of its own is a bedtime story to help us sleep. 'History as contingency is a prospect that is more than the human spirit can bear,' said Robert Heilbroner, the late American economist. For centuries, Westerners have taken a linear view of history, in which time is always marching us towards a happier place. The Greeks called it teleology. For Christians, it was the Second Coming of Christ and the Day of Judgement. For Marxists, it was the dictatorship of the proletariat followed by the withering away of the state. For European nationalists, it was seizing control of their Volk destiny. For Georgian and Victorian liberals on both sides of the Atlantic, and their modern heirs across the Western world, it was the progress of human liberty to individual freedom. In 1989 most people believed that last version. The others were either dead or in retreat. Today, only Marxism remains dormant. Belief in an authoritarian version of national destiny is staging a powerful comeback. Western liberalism is under siege.

More to the point, non-Western visions of history, which were overshadowed by colonial rule but never forgotten, are staking their pressing claim to relevance. In very different ways, China and India have traditionally taken a circular view of history. They still do. Material conditions may improve. But humanity's moral condition is constant. There is no spiritual or political finale towards which history is guiding us. To the rest of the world, which accounts for almost nine-tenths of humanity, most of whom are now finally starting to catch up with the West's material advantages, humankind's moral progress is a question that can never be settled. History does not end. It is a timeless repetition of human folly and correction. It follows that there is no single model of how to organise society. Who, barring those of religious faith, can say that view is wrong?

But the most mortal threat to the Western idea of progress comes from within. Donald Trump, and his counterparts in Europe, did not cause the crisis of democratic liberalism. They are a symptom. This may be hard to digest, particularly for

American liberals, whose worldview has been shaken by his victory yet who retain faith that things will eventually turn out fine. Many comfort themselves that Trump's victory was an accident delivered by the dying gasp of America's white majority – and abetted by Putin. History will resume normal business after a brief interruption. How I wish they were right. I fear they are not. Since the turn of the millennium, and particularly over the last decade, no fewer than twenty-five democracies have failed around the world, three of them in Europe (Russia, Turkey and Hungary). In all but Tunisia, the Arab Spring was swallowed by the summer heat. Is the Western god of liberal democracy failing? 'It is an open question whether this is a market correction in democracy, or a global depression,' Francis Fukuyama tells me.[4] The backlash of the West's middle classes, who are the biggest losers in a global economy that has been rapidly converging, but still has decades to go, has been brewing since the early 1990s. In Britain we call them the 'left-behinds'. In France, they are the 'couches moyennes'. In America, they are the 'squeezed middle'. A better term is the 'precariat' – those whose lives are dominated by economic insecurity. Their weight of numbers is growing. So, too, is their impatience. Barrington Moore, the American sociologist, famously said, 'No bourgeoisie, no democracy.' In the coming years we will find out if he was right.

This book is divided into four parts. The first, Fusion, explains the integration of the global economy and the radical impact that is having on Western economies. By any numerical measure, humanity is becoming rapidly less poor. But between half and two-thirds of people in the West have been treading water – at best – for a generation. Tens of millions of Westerners will struggle to keep their heads above the surface over the coming decades. The spread of automation, including artificial intelligence and remote intelligence, which some call the fourth industrial revolution, is still in its early stages. So too is what the American journalist Fareed Zakaria has labelled the rise of the rest.[5] The emergence of China is the most dramatic event in economic history. We are living in an age of convergence no less dramatic than the age of divergence brought about by European colonialism and the Industrial Revolution. The downward pressure on the incomes of the West's middle classes in the coming years will be relentless.

The second part, Reaction, explains the resulting degeneration of Western politics. We are taught to think our democracies are held together by values. Our faith in history fuels that myth. But liberal democracy's strongest glue is economic growth. When groups fight over the fruits of growth, the rules of the political game are relatively easy to uphold. When those fruits disappear, or are monopolised by a fortunate few, things turn nasty. History should have taught us that. The losers seek scapegoats. The politics of interest group management turn into a zero-sum battle over declining resources. The past also tells us to beware of the West at times of stark and growing inequality. It rarely ends well.

The third part, Fallout, explores the implications of declining US – and Western – hegemony. Though the US remains the most potent military power on earth, and its most technologically innovative, Americans are losing faith in their system. Donald Trump offers a cure worse than the disease. Moreover, Europe is turning inwards. As Henry Kissinger puts it, 'the United States, if separated from Europe in politics, economics and defense, would become geopolitically an island off the shores of Eurasia'.[6] I argue that chaos is far likelier than China to fill America's shoes.

The final section, Half Life, asks what is to be done. If you value individual liberty, as I do, then you should want to preserve the kind of society that allows it to flourish. It was part of the end-of-history narrative to believe that we had shed age-old human prejudices. In so doing we forgot what it took to contain them. What has changed is the public's trust that societies are all in this together, including the elites. That invisible referendum is the essence of the Western social contract. Identity liberalism – a politics that treats society as less than the sum of its parts – is partly to blame. It has helped to fuel a backlash by majority-white communities that are now borrowing the tactics of minority politics. We cannot progress without a clear-eyed grasp of what has gone wrong. Unless and until reeling Western establishments understand what is hitting them, they have little chance of saving liberalism from itself.

A health warning: journalists have a habit of labelling things, which is a trait they share with historians. While the latter take their time to brand the past – the age of steam, the rise of the West, the birth of the modern, and so on – journalists do so without drawing breath. It is in the nature of the business. We flatter ourselves that we rush out the first draft of history. My profession is thus liable to over-interpret the latest big thing. Moreover, we have an annoying habit of designating what we failed to predict as serenely inevitable in hindsight. It was destined to happen all along. I have been guilty of this. As you read these pages, please bear in mind that Brexit was not destined to happen. Holding the referendum was a rash throw of the dice by an instinctively tactical British prime minister. Nor was Trump's victory somehow inevitable. If seventy-seven thousand Midwestern votes had gone the other way Hillary Clinton would now be president. But it works both ways. Should Marine Le Pen lose the French presidential election and Angela Merkel hold on to power in Germany, or indeed, Martin Shultz, the SPD leader, take over from her, the crisis of Western liberalism will not have suddenly come to an end, though I suspect many of us would broadcast it as such. It was puzzling to hear many interpret the defeat of Norbert Hofer in the Austrian presidential election in December as a defeat for populism. Hofer took almost 47 per cent of the vote. If the narrow defeat of a right-wing nationalist qualified as breaking the populist wave, what would surfing it look like? Nor, for that matter, would America's future be secure if Mrs Clinton were now in the White House. The West's crisis is real, structural and likely to persist. Nothing is inevitable. Some of what ails the West is within our power to fix. Doing so means understanding exactly how we got here. It would also require a conscious effort to look at the world from unfamiliar standpoints and admit that the West has no monopoly on truth or virtue. In this book I do my best to avoid the pitfalls of my day job and address the larger forces that are upending our world: the urgent will cede to the very important – or that is my aim. So I propose a pact with the reader: if you take my pledge at face value, I will try to redeem it. My guess is it will take you roughly three hours.

PART ONE

FUSION

... the most imperious of all necessities, that of
not sinking in the world.

ALEXIS DE TOCQUEVILLE[1]

O n, or about, January 2017, the global economy changed guard. The venue was Davos, the annual gathering of the world's wealthiest recyclers of conventional wisdom – and consistently one of the last places to anticipate what is going to happen next. This time was different. The assembled hedge-fund tycoons, Silicon Valley data executives, management gurus and government officials were treated to a preview of how rapidly the world is about to change. Xi Jinping, the president of China, had come to the Swiss Alpine resort to defend the global trade system against the attacks of the newly elected US president, Donald Trump. With minimal fanfare, the leader of the world's largest developing economy took over the role of defending the global trading system in the teeth of protectionist war cries from the world's most developed nation. It portended a new era in which China would aspire to be the responsible global citizen. The bad guys were swapping places with the good. 'Some people blame economic globalisation for the chaos in our world,' Xi told Davos. 'We should not retreat into the harbour whenever we encounter a storm or we will never reach the other shore ... No one will emerge as a winner from a trade war.'

After more than seventy years of US-led globalisation, Xi's declaration of global stewardship in the spiritual home of capitalism was an Alice in Wonderland moment. Yet the switch in roles – the changing of the global economy's sentinel – had been widely predicted. Set aside the most recent forecasts. As far back as 1902, when China's imperial ruins had long since been picked over by the European powers and the United States, the British historian John Hobson anticipated the day when a resurgent China would turn the tables. Hobson's prescience is worth savouring: 'China, passing more quickly than other "lower races" through the period of dependence on Western science and Western capital, and quickly assimilating what they have to give, may re-establish her own economic independence finding out of her own resources the capital and organising skill required for the machine industries and ... may quickly launch herself upon the world-market as the biggest and most effective competitor, taking to herself first the trade of Asia and the Pacific, and then swamping the free markets of the West, and driving the closed markets of the West to an ever more rigorous Protection'.[2]

Though something of a Nostradamus, not even Hobson envisaged the speed with which China would pull this off. From barely a statistical rounding error in 1978, with less than 1 per cent of global trade, China rose to become in 2013 the world's leading trading nation with almost a quarter of its annual flows.[3] As recently as the turn of the twenty-first century, the US accounted for almost three times as much global trade as China. Nothing on this scale or speed has been witnessed before in history. Yet it still has a long way to go. The return of China, and the fifteen other fast-growing non-Western economies, including Indonesia, Thailand and India, which together account for half the world's population, is dramatically reconfiguring the global power structure. Within my lifetime, the emerging middle class has gone from virtually nowhere to supplant the established Western middle class as the engine of global growth. Since 1970, Asia's per-capita incomes have increased fivefold.[4] Even in Africa, the world's worst-performing continent, incomes have almost doubled. The West's median income, meanwhile, has barely shifted in the last half-century. In some parts of Asia, such as Singapore and South Korea, incomes have either overtaken or are level-pegging with the West. In others, notably India, they still languish at less than a tenth of the Western average. But the direction is clear. If you chart a global economic map, the centre of gravity in the twentieth century could be found somewhere in the mid-Atlantic, according to the Singaporean economist Danny Quah. That point has now shifted eastwards to Iran.[5] Over the coming decades it will settle at a point somewhere between China and India, in the Himalayas.

From the middle of the Atlantic to the roof of the world in fifty years – our generation is present at the re-creation.

Yet this will only restore China to the relative weight it has enjoyed for most of human history. For roughly seven centuries, between 1100, shortly after the Norman Conquest, and 1800, when the Industrial Revolution took off, China accounted for roughly a quarter of the global economy – and an even higher share of its estimated production. By one recent historical measure, China and India in 1750 produced three-quarters of the world's manufactures. On the eve of the First World War their share had dropped to just 7.5 per cent.[6] Economic historians called it the Age of Divergence. Much of the East's sharp decline – perhaps too much – has been blamed on the direct effects of colonial exploitation. The British East India Company, for example, suppressed Indian textile production, which had led the world. Indian silks were displaced by Lancashire cotton. Chinese porcelain was supplanted by European 'china'. Both suffered from variations on what Britain later called Imperial Preference, which forced them to export low-value raw materials to Britain, and import expensive finished products, thus keeping them in permanent deficit. There was nothing *free* about such trade in any sense of the word. In China's case, the Western powers each wrested their own concessions that enabled them to do much the same thing in China as the British were doing in India – but without nationwide garrisons. The impact was similar. Again, Hobson captured it starkly: '[The] investors and business managers of the West appear to have struck in China a mine of labour power . . . it seems so enormous and so expansible as to open up the possibility of raising whole white populations of the West to the position of "independent gentlemen".[7]

The debate about the West's moral debt to its former colonies is often too one-sided. Those who point to Britain's extraction of wealth from India, for example, tend to overlook the impact of social reforms that for the first time gave benighted lower-caste Indians the chance to read and write, or that protected upper-caste widows from *sati*, where they were expected to throw themselves onto their husband's funeral pyre. There is no moral abacus that can settle the pros and cons of each instance of colonialism. In the case of slavery, no debate is necessary. The African slave trade was a crime against humanity in which Britain and America played starring roles. But Europe's economic success was chiefly driven by technological superiority rather than by a fit of immoral looting.

From the Opium Wars of the 1840s until the 1949 communist revolution, China's century of humiliation still rankles – and in some respects its historic resentment appears to be deepening. But the fact that the Industrial Revolution took place in Europe, rather than in Asia, played a more critical role in China's fall from grace than the often-sordid tale of Western exploitation. China and India were not so much drained of wealth – though much of that took place – as they were rapidly overtaken by the West's superior machine. Asia's latter-day exploitation would not have been possible without the West's development of steam power, advanced military technology, new financial techniques and modern organisational skills. These were the prime movers. In 1820, Britain had a per-capita income of $2000 in today's prices. That had risen to $5000 by the eve of the First World War. Over the same period, China's income dipped from $600 a head to $550, while India's edged up from $600 to $700.[8] In absolute terms, Asia's economic conditions barely shifted. In relative weight, Asia shrank dramatically. Just as nothing in history compares to today's Great Convergence, there was no precedent for the West's vertiginous rise two centuries ago that launched the Great Divergence.

Modernity was born in the West. Ask educated Westerners today why it was their part of the world, rather than another continent, that wrote the rules of the modern age, and they will likely tell you of Europe's scientific revolution and the Enlightenment – and possibly the Renaissance. That would be true, as far as it goes. But history is more complicated than the stories we learn in school. What most would be unlikely to know is the degree to which Chinese technology provided critical sparks to the Industrial Revolution. Among other techniques and inventions, Europe took far-superior iron and steel production; the printing press; navigational tools, including the compass; gunpowder; and paper money from China. From Islam, Europe took binary mathematics (originally from India), astronomy, double-entry bookkeeping and much of its own forgotten knowledge

24

from classical Greece and Rome. '[Much] of the European revival was based on the ideas, institutions, and technologies borrowed from the advanced civilizations in the Middle and Far East,' notes Richard Baldwin, whose book on today's Great Convergence is rightly acclaimed.[9] The shift of power from the Islamic world to the Christian in the late Middle Ages had, in turn, been enabled by the destructive westward sweep of Genghis Khan's Mongol hordes in the thirteenth century. In addition to its more benign exports, Mongol China delivered the Black Death, which wiped out between a third and a half of Europe's population within three years. Here, too, the impact was complex. As the more urban civilisation, the Islamic world was dealt an even worse fate by the bubonic plague, since its people were more concentrated and so more exposed than those in Europe. You could say that the Mongols sharply improved Europe's terms of trade. Jeffrey Garten's history of globalisation, *From Silk to Silicon*, tells the story of the last millennium through ten biographies. His book ends with Steve Jobs. It opens with Genghis Khan. The latter's impact was a fitting one with which to begin his story.

What does history tell us to expect from China's resurgence in the years ahead? 'If we take the long view,' writes Hugh White, Australia's leading Sinologist, 'the rise of India and China today is less a revolution than a restoration – a return to normal after a two-century interlude.'[10] During the 1990s and the early 2000s, American policy-makers exhaustively debated how to respond to China's rise. No one was quite sure whether China would become a partner of the US, or turn into an adversary. Washington settled on a hedging strategy of accommodating China's self-proclaimed peaceful rise while retaining the option of switching to containment if it turned sour. What has never been in question is that America will do what it takes to preserve its primacy in the Asia Pacific. The prevailing American view in the 1990s was that China's economic interdependence with the rest of the world would reduce the risk of war by raising its price. Besides, China's economy was simply too big to shut out. In arguing for its entry to the World Trade Organization, Bill Clinton, the then US president, said globalisation was 'the economic equivalent of a force of nature, like wind or water'. In addition, he argued that China's entry would reduce America's bilateral trade deficit by binding China to lower tariff rates on its imports. Following China's WTO accession in 2001, America's trade deficit with China has leapt almost five-fold. It is clear, in retrospect, that Beijing had a better grasp of the global economy's dynamics than Washington.

China has profited beyond its wildest hopes from the club it joined, and now offers to cheerlead. Whether the global trading system remains open will depend on the actions of the West's increasingly reactive democracies. Xi Jinping and his peers can bank on the support of their largest foreign investors, the multinational companies that have located large chunks of their production supply chains in China and other parts of the Asia Pacific. In today's world, most cross-border trade is intra-company movement of unfinished goods. Apple's iPhone is produced in nine different countries. Since the goal is to capture Western technology, it makes no sense for developing countries to slap tariffs on imports, which are as likely to be intermediate goods moving from one part of the supply chain to the next. Baldwin calls this process of productive unbundling a fractionalised world. It differs greatly from the old factory model in which all a product's components were made in one location. Xi's best allies are thus the global chief executives who came to hear him in Davos. All dread the wrath of an alienated Western middle class.

Economists are notorious for getting the future wrong (just as they are peerless at explaining the past). The joke is that they have predicted ten out of the last five recessions. In recent years, during what is now called the age of hyper-globalisation, bad forecasting has erred in the opposite direction. Economists have consistently predicted growth where none has materialised. In particular, since the 2008 global financial crisis, forecasts have annually over-estimated the next year's growth. The quickest way to verify this is to leaf through each of the past eight years' estimates of the Davos Forum's Global Economic Outlook.[11] But if you stand back, the longer trends are unmistakable. China may well have to grapple with its own recession in the coming years (I can safely forecast that Western journalists would then promptly declare the death of China's miracle). Indeed, Beijing ought already to have engineered a recession given the country's high levels of domestic debt. At some point it will need to liquidate its bad loans. But China's politburo clearly dreads the domestic backlash a recession might trigger. It has thus opted for slower growth – preferring to let the air out of the balloon rather than pop it.

Whatever its short-term fortunes, China will continue to make big strides on the West in the coming decades. In terms of purchasing power parity – measured by what you can buy in the local currency – China's economy surpassed the US in 2014.[12] Within a decade, give or take a few years, China will overtake America on more conventional dollar measures. By 2050 – a century after its communist revolution – China's economy is likely to be twice the size of America's and larger than all the Western economies combined. A century of restoration will have followed the century of humiliation. And by then, India's economy will be roughly the same size as America's. Whether the Western way of life, and our liberal democratic systems, can survive this dramatic shift of global power is the question of this book. The answer is not entirely in our hands. But our response so far has been to accelerate the shift. Donald Trump's victory crystallises the West's failure to come to terms with the reality it faces.

––––––––

At some point during the 2008 global financial crisis, the Washington Consensus died. In truth, that economic model had been declared a 'damaged brand' back in 2003 by John Williamson, the man who coined the term in the late 1980s.[13] The Washington Consensus prescribed open trading systems, free movement of capital and central bank monetary discipline. Countries that swallowed the prescription suffered terribly during the 1995 Mexican tesobono crisis, the 1997 Asian flu crisis, and in Russia, Brazil and elsewhere during the later 1990s. The Organization for Economic Cooperation and Development, the prestigious Western club that was set up to distribute America's Marshall Plan aid to shattered post-war Europe, made capital account liberalisation a precondition of its membership. Everyone wanted to join the OECD for its prestige and higher credit ratings. South Korea and Mexico duly liberalised their capital accounts to join in the early 1990s. The destabilising effects of the hot money that flooded into those economies and then out again was almost instant. Most of the world has since chosen China's more pragmatic path of opening slowly and on its own terms. China's unorthodox route to development exposed the limits of the Washington Consensus. It had assumed that there was one way to do things, and that the rest of the world would have little choice but to adopt it. China is simply too big, and too important to the world's bottom line, to push around. Other developing countries have followed China's cue. Call it the Beijing Consensus.

Today we still reflexively call the meltdown that followed the bankruptcy of Lehman Brothers a global recession. But that is quite wrong. It was an Atlantic recession. In 2009, China's economy grew by almost 10 per cent, and India's by almost 8 per cent. The Western economies contracted. As is so often the case, our ways of thinking about the world lag behind reality. The most important example of this is how we think about economic growth in the West. We still measure our health in aggregate numbers. But averages are useless. As Robert H. Frank, the Cornell economist, points out, on average we have about 1.9 legs each, because some people have only one leg.[14] Likewise, if Mark Zuckerberg joins your neighbourhood football team, every member is on average a billionaire.

Under the old model, where most production was clustered behind national barriers, what was good for General Motors was good for America. The annual gross domestic product figure meant as much to GM's American customers as it did to the company. If the US economy grew by 5 per cent, there was a high chance the auto-maker's bottom line had expanded by a similar amount. America's median income growth rose in line with GDP. Much the same could have been said of Britain's ICI, or Rolls-Royce. That is an outmoded way of measuring growth in today's world. Since 2009, the US economy has expanded by roughly 2 per cent a year. Yet it took until 2015 for the median income to regain the level it enjoyed before the Great Recession. Perhaps 'enjoyed' is the wrong word. The median income in

2007 was below what it was in 2002, at the start of the business cycle that lasted for most of George W. Bush's presidency. What is good for Apple may not be good for America. It shuttered its last US production facility in 2004. The Bush expansion was the first on record where middle-class incomes were lower at the end of it than at the start. Today, the US median income is still below where it was at the beginning of this century. Clearly what the typical American understands by growth differs greatly from that of macroeconomists. GDP numbers insist we are doing well, at a time when half the country is suffering from personal recessions.

The world's most informative graph is the Elephant Chart. Devised by Branko Milanovic, a former World Bank staffer, this statistical pachyderm has many virtues. It is intuitively simple and tells you pretty much everything you need to know about the era of high globalisation since the fall of the Berlin Wall. It shows the distribution of more than two decades of growth between different percentiles of the global economy. The global median – the emerging middle classes of China, Vietnam, India and so on – enjoyed income growth of more than 80 per cent in those years. Even the bottom deciles, in Africa and South Asia, saw growth of up to 50 per cent. The key part of the elephant for the Western middle classes is where its trunk slopes downwards – between the seventy-fifth and ninetieth percentiles of the world's population. These account for the majority of the West's people. At their mid-point, incomes grew by a grand total of *1 per cent* over the last three decades. The original chart ended in 2008. In that short period since the 'global' recession, China's urban incomes had already doubled. The bulging frame of the elephant only includes some of the developing world. Many other regions, including most of Africa, Bangladesh, Central Asia and corners of Andean South America, have yet to contribute noticeably to the elephant's bulk. Their absorption is a matter of time. In much the same way that Western investment helped bring China into the global system, Chinese investment is now doing the same for Africa and elsewhere. As China's wages rise, its demand for cheaper labour grows. The Western worker is painfully familiar with the story. The long-term portents for Western standards of living are disturbing. 'If this wave of globalization is holding back the income growth of the rich world's middle classes, what will be the result of the next wave, involving ever-poorer and more populous countries, such as Bangladesh, Burma, and Ethiopia?' asks Milanovic.[15]

The last part of the elephant is the tip of its trunk, which shoots straight upwards in a suitably celebratory posture. That is the global top 1 per cent. Their incomes have jumped by more than two-thirds over the same period. But as Milanovic shows, that would be dramatically to understate the bonanza the global 1 per cent – who are still mostly to be found in the West – have reaped since the start of the Great Convergence. The top 1 per cent's share of the global economy is 15.7 per cent. But if you measure their net wealth, and provide reasonable estimates of what they have salted away in hidden corners, such as the offshore financial havens of the Caribbean and elsewhere, their share jumps to almost a third of global wealth. The nearer the snout you get, the sharper the growth. The world's wealthiest subset – the 1426 richest individuals on the planet – are worth $5.4 trillion, which is roughly twice the size of the entire British economy and more than the combined assets of the 250 million least wealthy Americans. The asset value of the world's leading billionaires has risen fivefold since 1988. What one could do with all that money is a parlour game we all enjoy: 'Suppose now that you inherited either $1 million or $1 billion, and that you spent $1000 every day. It would take you less than three years to run through your inheritance in the first case, and more than 2700 years (that is, the time that separates us from Homer's *Iliad*) to blow your inheritance in the second case,' says Milanovic of the richest group. Meanwhile, between a quarter and a third of people in the West have negative or zero net wealth. They face penurious retirements. As I say, if you want an economic chart that stops you from sleeping you should start with the elephant.

Now, recall what came before the elephant. That was what we now refer to as the Golden Age of Western middle-class growth between the late 1940s and the early 1970s, or what the French call *les Trente Glorieuses* of rising incomes for the bulk of society. The annual gains were almost metronomic. Then something went wrong. It can be corrected, we tell ourselves. The West somehow managed to step off the natural escalator that assured annual income growth of 2 to 3 per cent, which roughly doubled our standard of living every generation or faster. We had faith that by the end of their lives our children would be three to four times better off than we are. For brief moments, such as during the internet boom of the 1990s, that age looked like it had returned. But the growth vanished almost as quickly as it came. We are still awaiting the productivity gains we were assured would result from the digital economy. With the exception of most of the 1990s, productivity growth has never recaptured the rates it achieved in the post-war decades. 'You can see the computer age everywhere but in the productivity statistics,' said Robert Solow, the Nobel Prize-winning economist. Peter Thiel, the Silicon Valley billionaire, who has controversially backed Donald Trump, put it more vividly: 'We wanted flying cars, instead we got 140 characters [Twitter].' That may be about to change, with the acceleration of the robot revolution and the spread of artificial intelligence. But we should be careful what we wish for. The squeeze is already uncomfortable enough.

I am nearing fifty. My generation – those born in the mid-to-late 1960s and the 1970s – straddled the transition from the golden years to the new normal, though we did not wake up to it until we were into our thirties. We grew up with the lofty expectations of our parents, but with the waning hope they would come to pass. The same is even more harshly true of our downgraded retirement prospects. To be clear: the West's souring mood is about the psychology of dashed expectations rather than the decline in material comforts. A few years ago a *New Yorker* cartoon caught the essence of how we feel about things. It showed a Chinese mother finger-wagging at her daughter's uneaten dinner: 'Eat your rice, Han Ling, don't you know there are children in West Virginia who are starving?' Nevertheless, most Westerners of almost any age group, and in almost any income bracket, are still considerably better off than most of their counterparts in China, India and other swathes of the emerging world – though those gaps are narrowing. (China's urban per-capita income is approaching half of the level of America's per-capita income. A generation ago it was a sixth.[16]) We are also unimaginably luckier than any generation before us. Queen Victoria would envy the medical care that is now free at point of access to even the most socially excluded UK citizen. Andrew Carnegie would marvel at the electronic library that is just a thumbprint away from all but the most disconnected Americans.

Are we simply imagining our woes? No. The West's middle-income problem is real and deepening. The most crushing effect is stagnation. Many of the tools of modern life are increasingly priced beyond most people's reach. Robert H. Frank monitors something called the Toil Index – the number of working hours it takes a median worker to pay the median rent in one of

America's big cities. In 1950 it took forty-five hours per month. A generation later it had edged up to fifty-six hours. Today it takes 101 hours.[17] Much the same rising unaffordability applies to the cost of decent health insurance in America, and higher education. If 1985 equals one hundred, then the price of most things, such as food, electronic goods, basic clothes or a car, has fallen to double digits, and in some cases astonishingly lower. These are the products you find on Walmart's shelves. In contrast, the cost of obtaining a degree, or paying for a reasonable package of health insurance, has catapulted to above six hundred.[18] The US rate of inflation has been hovering around 1 per cent for years. Yet the cost of services that will enable people to survive and their children to thrive is growing at double-digit annual rates. Inflation is another outdated number that no longer means much to the typical Westerner. It no longer captures what people most value. Without good health and the ability to pick up the cognitive skills you will need to get a good job in tomorrow's economy, your life chances are badly handicapped. This is not an outgrowth of people's frustrated imaginations. It is what many, and possibly most, Westerners experience on a daily basis. The runaway costs of acquiring social capital are why so many are so pessimistic about their children's life prospects.

When people lose faith in the future they are less likely to invest in the present. That sense of personal stagnation – and the gnawing fear you may even be sinking – casts an enervating pall over the human spirit. Ronald Reagan once said, 'Progress is our most important product.' He was speaking of General Electric, for whom he worked. But he also meant America. Writing in the 1950s, Daniel Bell, the great American sociologist, said, 'economic growth has become the secular religion of advancing industrial societies'. He was right. It follows that in its absence, many people lapse into the equivalent of atheism. That sense of listlessness shows up in many ways. In the labour market, it means falling rates of workforce participation. Much as the desire to worship falls in agnostic societies, the yen to work drops in flat economies. In the last decade, America's share of people in full-time jobs has dropped to European levels, which used to be written off as a sclerotic consequence of the continent's over-regulated labour markets. Now the US rate is bang on the European average. In some respects it is worse. There is now a higher share of French males in full-time jobs than Americans – a statistic that reflects poorly on America, rather than well on France.[19]

America's opioid epidemic is another warning light. Émile Durkheim, the father of modern sociology, said that when societies hit a civilisational break the suicide rate soars. Deaths from drug overdoses have tripled since 2000: America's opioid-heroin epidemic now rivals HIV-Aids at its peak. Some of the deaths are accidental. Some deliberate. You can choose your culprit. Heroin comes from Mexico. Painkillers come from your family doctor. The epidemic's rise is linked to the rapid spread of prescription painkillers. America's incidence of acute pain has not quadrupled since the late 1990s, yet the volume of painkiller prescriptions has. Sales of OxyContin, the strongest opioid on the market, shot up from $45 million in 1995 to $3.1 billion in 2015.[20] The epidemic is one reason US life expectancy has dipped in recent years,[21] which is not supposed to happen in peacetime. Other symptoms of stagnation include falling tolerance for other people's point of view, and a fading enthusiasm to join social groups. 'I believe that the rising intolerance and incivility and the eroding generosity and openness that have marked important aspects of American society in the recent past have been, in significant part, a consequence of the stagnation of American middle-class living standards,' writes Ben Friedman, in the The Moral Consequences of Economic Growth.[22] De Tocqueville talked admiringly of America's 'restlessness of temper'. Today, in a society where Americans are increasingly 'bowling alone', as Robert Putnam put it, the great French chronicler might be moved to talk about America's shortness of temper. Adam Smith, the great theorist of free trade economics, is revered for his The Wealth of Nations. His companion work, The Theory of Moral Sentiments, is mostly forgotten. Yet it is the more important of the two. In it, Smith sets out why capitalism works best in societies where there are high levels of trust between its participants. When social trust falls, the cost of doing business rises. Even in the late eighteenth century, at the dawn of modern growth, Smith grasped the psychological importance of possessing faith in a better future. When trust goes, so much else goes with it. '[It] is in the progressive state, while the society is advancing to the further acquisition, rather than when it has acquired its full complement of riches, that the condition of the labouring poor, of the great body of the people, seems to be the happiest and the most comfortable,' Smith wrote.[23]

When economic growth slows, society loses pace. That might seem counterintuitive in an age of instant connectivity. But we delude ourselves that the frequency with which we post Facebook updates, tweet or communicate on Snapchat amounts to meaningful action. Having hundreds of Facebook friends is no substitute for seeing people. Western societies are steadily getting older. The median age in the US is now thirty-nine compared with twenty-seven in India, for example. In the UK it is forty.[24] During the baby boom years, which ended in 1964, people tended to have large families, as is true today for most of the rising middle classes in Asia and elsewhere. An ageing society is a less entrepreneurial one. Americans are far less likely to move across state boundaries than their parents. Interstate migration has fallen by more than half since its peak in the post-war decades. Older societies are also less likely to launch businesses. The rate of start-ups in America has been dropping for years and is beginning to rival Europe's less entrepreneurial pace. America's per-capita rate of triadic patent applications – those that are filed in the US, Europe and Japan, which screens out the frivolous ones – has fallen by a quarter since 2000.[25]

The fastest-growing units in the big Western companies are the legal and public relations departments. Big companies devote the bulk of their earnings to buying back shares and boosting dividend payments. They no longer invest anything like what they used to in research and development. The future loses out. Tyler Cowen, who is perhaps the most lateral-thinking economist I know, talks of the rise of America's 'complacent classes' – the creep of a risk-averse and conformist mindset. In a supposed age of hyper-individualism, eccentricity is penalised. Software screens out job applicants before they have a chance to show their faces. Matchmaking algorithms do the same for our love lives. Cowen detects conformism even in the liveliest Silicon Valley companies. Most of its denizens wear some variation on the casual hipster uniform and all dutifully strip the paint off their office walls. They litter their workplaces with the same multicoloured pouffes. 'We are using the acceleration of information transmission to decelerate changes in our physical world,' writes Cowen. 'Most Americans [today] do not like change very much unless it is something they can manage and control.'[26] The same applies in spades to Europe. The biggest 'ideological carriers' of the new complacency are the millennials, he says. It follows that they are therefore the least angry generation in society. In spite of having grown up in relatively straitened circumstances, Westerners born since 1981 do not suffer the same inflated expectations as their elders. Millennials have grown up with something the rest of us may be forced to learn in the years ahead.

These are the costs, both material and psychological, that we pay for stagnation. The other big crisis of Western political economy is rising income inequality. The West is suffering from acute polarisation. History tells us that inequality soars when societies develop. That is what economic theory dictates as well. During the nineteenth century, British and US inequality rose to giddying heights as the owners of new wealth – the railroads, shipping lines, iron and steel mills and machine industries – reaped the benefits of vast new monopolies. It was also an age of ferment. Though wealth gaps reached almost biblical levels in the era of robber barons, people were on the move. British farm labourers uprooted almost wholesale from the countryside to the factories. America's land poor extended the western frontier. And Europeans of all nationalities crossed the Atlantic in search of a better life. Europe had too many people and too little land. The US suffered the opposite imbalance. Between 1880 and 1890, during one of the West's periodic depressions, more than 2 per cent of each of the populations of Italy, Sweden, Germany, Ireland and Britain made the passage to America.[27] That sheer weight of late-Victorian movement has only been rivalled in recent decades by the internal migrations that have convulsed China, India and elsewhere. Uprooting is what happens when societies reinvent their means of production. People go to where the money is.

Both history and theory told us that the rising inequalities created by industrialisation would be followed by the strong forces of equalisation as societies became richer. In the newly created Germany, Otto von Bismarck set up the world's first social insurance system for the working classes in the late nineteenth century. Britain followed suit under Lloyd George in the early twentieth century. America distributed small parcels of freeholdings to first-comers in the feverish westwards push that came after the Civil War. Had America instead chosen to auction the undivided land to the highest bidders, the US would now have a Latin American-style *hacienda* economy. The railroad barons would have gobbled up most of the land and converted it into vast estates.[28] America also made public land grants to set up new universities across its rapidly opening landscape. Each of the big Western countries consciously opted to spread skills and assets to its poor. For the first time in history, governments extended public education, moving the school leaving age upwards as the factory clock supplanted the farm day as the timekeeper of the new age. The gilded age was an era of spectacular new wealth. It was also a time of conscious improvement for the masses. They were no longer unlettered. As China and India are discovering, the rise of mass literacy changes everything. Though the Rowntrees and the Carnegies became richer than God, their workers could read and write. Andrew Carnegie spent much of his fortune building libraries across the US, and in Scotland, the land of his birth. Perhaps he took it a little too far. 'Do not pauperize the poor man further,' Carnegie tells his butler of a beggar asking for bread in a newspaper cartoon, 'give him a library.'

The golden decades of the post-war era bore out the theory of declining inequality. But over the last thirty years that has gone into reverse. During those decades, the share of the US economic pie divided between labour and capital was roughly 70:30.[29] Capital's share – the flows taken up by returns on financial assets rather than wages and salaries – has since risen to a level not seen since the days of *The Great Gatsby*. The gap between the pay of the average chief executive and their employees has risen tenfold since the late 1970s to around four hundred.[30] Europe has seen varying rates of rising inequality, with Britain and Spain recording the fastest-rising Gini coefficient – the measure of inequality – and Germany and Scandinavia the least. But all have been moving the same way. In contrast to the industrial era, however, today's inequality is accompanied by vanishing mobility. It is not just that people are staying physically put. They are also likelier to stay trapped in the same income group. America, in particular, which had traditionally shown the highest class mobility of any Western country, now has the lowest. Today it is rarer for a poor American to become rich than a poor Briton, which means the American dream is less likely to be realised in America.[31] The meritocratic society has given way to a hereditary meritocracy. The children of the rich are overwhelmingly likely to stay rich. In place of churning, we have stasis. To a large extent, your life chances have been set by the time you are five. '[If] you want to be smart and highly energetic, the most important single step you could take is to choose the right parents,' says Robert Frank.[32] Alas, in today's West, too many people are choosing the wrong parents.

What is in a word? When it is packed with as much moral zeal as 'meritocracy', the answer is a great deal. A meritocrat owes his success to effort and talent. Luck has nothing to do with it – or so he tells himself. He shares his view with everyone else, including those too slow or indolent to follow his example. Things only go wrong when the others dispute it. Now magnify that to a nation of 324 million people, one that prides itself on being a land of opportunity. Imagine that between a half and two-thirds of its people, depending on how the question is framed, disagree. They believe the system's divisions are self-perpetuating. They used not to think that way. Imagine, also, that the meritocrats are too enamoured of their just rewards to see it. Sooner or later something will give. An exaggeration? About a third of legacy applicants – those whose parent attended – are accepted into Harvard. Richard Reeves of the Brookings Institution calls them 'dream hoarders'.[33] Judged by aptitude, almost half those in America's top two-fifths income bracket are there because of the luck of family background. Think of the value of those unpaid internships and family connections. Think of what those pricy weekend tutors did for your prospects. A big share of those in the bottom fifth would be in the top if they had the same life chances. According to one Harvard study, more students attended America's elite universities from the top 1 per cent of income backgrounds than from the bottom 60 per cent.[34] About one in four of the richest Americans attended an elite university, compared with less than half of 1 per cent of the bottom fifth. By far the biggest determinant is the bed in which you were born. Why wouldn't the losers be angry?

There are more of them than there used to be. In 2000, exactly a third of Americans described themselves as lower class, according to Gallup. By 2015 that number had risen to almost half.[35] Far from withering away, as we expected would happen, the working class is growing in leaps and bounds according to people's self-perception. In many ways these self-identification surveys mean much more than hard statistics on median income or income inequality. They express a feeling people have about being shut out from society. It is a very un-American state of mind. As is true of most of these trends, the West's drift to pessimism has been most radical in the land of optimism. Michael Young, the British sociologist who coined the term meritocracy in his 1958 book *The Rise of the Meritocracy*, would feel vindicated. Though the word soon lost its irony, Young meant it as a satire on the imagined ruling classes of the future. Meritocratic elites 'can be insufferably smug', he said in a 2001 critique of Prime Minister Tony Blair's misuse of the word.[36] The rest, meanwhile, 'can easily become demoralised by being looked down on so woundingly by people who have done well for themselves'. Young forecast that his meritocratic society would break down under the weight of its own contradictions by 2033. Events may be moving faster than that. Little wonder the tone of our politics has shifted so markedly from hope to nostalgia.[37]

Unlike during the early Industrial Revolution, today's poor are not intentionally being displaced. Instead they are being silently priced out of their homes. They are falling victim to creeping gentrification, or what Spike Lee, the American film-maker, calls 'the motherfuckin' Christopher Columbus Syndrome'.[38] In the US they call this reverse white flight, as the offspring of the suburban well-to-do reclaim the downtown wards and boroughs their parents and grandparents fled in the post-war era. The term gentrification was coined by Ruth Glass, a British academic, who was commenting on an early version of the trend in 1960s London. Today, no single London borough has a working-class majority. More of Britain's poor live in suburbia, or 'slumburbia', than in the cities nowadays.[39] This is creating a new kind of poverty, where the poor are increasingly pushed out of sight. This physical segregation matches the labour market's bifurcation. The rich and the poor no longer live near each other, and the middle class is hollowing out. In 1970 only about one in seven American families lived in neighbourhoods that were unambiguously 'affluent' or 'poor'.[40] By 2007 that number had risen to almost one in three. 'When all is said and done, the suburban crisis reflects the end of the era of cheap growth,' says Richard Florida, a leading scholar of urban revival.[41] Sprawl no longer means growth, as it once did in the US. It spells isolation. It should come as little surprise, therefore, that the murder rate has fallen by 16.7 per cent in the US cities since the turn of the century, while rising by 16.9 per cent in the suburbs – almost an exact mirror image.[42] Slumburbia has also given rise to a new form of poverty: the amount of time people have to spend in their cars driving from one part-time job to another. The more time you waste in traffic, the likelier you are to suffer from hypertension, diabetes, stress and obesity. A life spent in the car is bad for your life expectancy. As we have seen, it can also play havoc with your political state of mind.

The West's metropolises are in the midst of a grand renaissance. These are the knowledge hubs and global cities that have more in common with their international counterparts than with their national hinterlands. Anyone who doubted this was disabused in 2016. Almost two-thirds of London voted to stay in the European Union. The rest of England and Wales disagreed. In spite of being home to fewer than one in seven people in Britain, London accounts for almost a third of its gross domestic product. Similarly, every single one of America's 493 wealthiest counties, almost all of them urban, voted for Hillary Clinton.[43] The remaining 2623 counties, most of them suburban or small-town, went for Donald Trump. The gap between the West's cities and the rest is perhaps the purest manifestation of the new divisions. Today, Chicago, like London, sucks in the best talent from its interior in the Midwest, where the swing to Trump was strongest. In the past, Chicago acted as a regional locomotive, buying the Midwest's farm produce and other raw commodities and then converting them into products. The city was linked to its surrounding geography and vice versa. Now it mostly hovers above its hinterlands. In some ways it is also parasitic on them.[44]

Much like the giant sucking sound of London hoovering up the UK's talent, Chicago now takes the best and the brightest from the small towns of America and plugs them into the global economy. Chicago's success is no longer symbiotic with its rural neighbours. It comes at their expense. Like London, Chicago's erstwhile middle classes also find it increasingly hard to keep up with rising costs. As the most educated people move to global cities, those with fewer qualifications find themselves shut out. The newly risen global cities outside the West, such as Dubai, overcome this problem by importing labour from poorer countries and putting them on visas that can be annulled at short notice. Western cities, such as London and Chicago, have no such luxury. In 2011, Boris Johnson, then London's mayor, saw the downside when the capital's fringes went on the rampage for several days, smashing up shops and burning cars, looting what they could not have. Five years later Britain's left-behinds vetoed London's economic interests in the Brexit referendum. To the West's economic losers, cities like London and Chicago are not so much magnets as death stars.

One of the ironies of the West's booming cities is how much lip service its more fortunate denizens pay to a progressive world-view. We really couldn't ask for a nicer elite. Yet the effects of how they spend their money are hardly progressive. For all the emphasis we place on our multicultural cities, they epitomise our oligarchic reality. In the US, the more liberal a city's politics, the higher the rate of inequality.[45] The most glaring examples, such as San Francisco and New York, are demonised by conservatives as citadels of far-left politics. Bill de Blasio, mayor of New York, was elected after railing against this 'tale of two cities'. Yet he has made almost no dent in its economic divide. De Blasio's efforts to date illustrate how difficult it is to swim against the economic tide. He offered new luxury apartment blocks in New York a tax break and other write-offs if they devoted a share of their space to affordable units for the less well off. The first such project, in Manhattan's Lincoln Square, was built with a separate entrance for its lower-floor occupants, which was quickly dubbed the 'poor door'.[46] Though the developers pocketed the tax breaks, their richer occupants preferred to maintain a system of social apart-heid. Occupants of the social housing units were not just forced to enter the tower separately. They were also denied access to its gym, swimming pool and other amenities. In San Francisco, an ideas factory for America's most liberal social policies, more than six in ten homes are now worth more than $1 million. As Richard Florida says, 'In the US your ZIP code is increasingly your destiny.' It will be interesting to see if Sadiq Khan, who was elected London's mayor on an inclusive mandate just weeks before the Brexit referendum, has better luck than Bill de Blasio. The odds are against him.

The jobs market offers a snapshot of rising inequality. The fastest-rising area of blue-collar jobs growth is the security industry – the private guards, police and other uniformed occupations that keep the wealthy neighbourhoods safe. The share of the labour force employed in this industry, which also includes prison guards, has risen by almost a third since the 1990s.[47] In America, the increase has been even sharper. Western cities are also where the world's billionaires choose to park their resources. New York has 116 billionaires. London has fifty-one. Los Angeles has fifty.[48] Many of them only live there part-time. As the city's essential workers, its senior police officers and school heads are priced out of town, they are replaced by wealthy cosmopolitans who divide their lives between different locations. The number of unoccupied apartments in New York rose by almost three-quarters at the turn of the century to thirty-four thousand in 2011.[49] London has witnessed similar growth. The new residents then lock in their gains by restricting land use, which keeps values high. Richard Florida calls them the 'new urban Luddites', who exploit an 'enormous and complex thicket of zoning laws and other land use regulations' to keep the others out. Tyler Cowen has coined a new acronym to replace Nimbys (Not in My Backyard): Bananas (Build Absolutely Nothing Anywhere Near Anything).[50]

Such risk aversion breeds its own failure. So deeply rooted is gentrification that Richard Florida has now modified his widely acclaimed thesis about the rise of the creative classes. Cities are becoming too successful for their own good. Until recently, he believed they would be the engine rooms of the new economy, embracing the diversity necessary to attract talent. That has certainly happened. Gay pride parades seem to get larger every year. A thousand multicultural flowers are blooming. Yet in squeezing out income diversity, the new urban economies are also shutting off the scope for serendipity. The West's global cities are like tropical islands surrounded by oceans of resentment. Florida's latest book is called *The New Urban Crisis*. Rather than being shaped by those who live there full-time, the characters of our biggest cities are increasingly driven by the global super-rich as a place to park their money. Many of the creative classes are being edged out. Urban down-towns have turned into 'deadened trophy districts'. New York's once-bohemian SoHo is now better known for its high-end boutiques than its artists' studios. SoHo could nowadays be found in any big city in the world. 'Superstar cities and tech hubs will become so expensive that they will turn into gilded and gated communities,' Florida predicts.[51] 'Their innovative and creative sparks will eventually fade.' Karl Marx was wrong: it is the rich who are losing their nation, not the proletariat. The gap between global cities and their national anchors is already a metaphor for our times. By contrast, the rise of the robot economy has only half lodged itself in our expectations. It is easy to dismiss some of Silicon Valley's wilder talk as the stuff of science-fiction movies. But the gap between sci-fi and reality is closing. The latter-day effects of globalisation have shaken Western solidarity. The future of artificial intelligence poses challenges that are likely to be orders of magnitude greater.

————

One of the bedtime stories we tell ourselves is that technology is everybody's friend. Given time, the machines will eventually work for all of us. To be sure, great leaps of efficiency, such as the mechanisation of agriculture, cause painful uprootings for huge numbers of people. We know that. But society always adjusts. Just as the buggy driver found work in a factory, or the farmhand reinvented herself as an office assistant, so the digital revolution will create new types of job to replace those it is destroying. History tells us this. As does economic theory. So lull yourself back to sleep. There are benign forces at work.

It is a refrain we should treat with deep scepticism. It is possible to imagine we can pull together to ensure that everyone will have a stake in a hyper-automated future. But there are gaping holes in this pleasant reverie. The digital revolution is still in its infancy, yet we are already throwing our toys out of the pram. As political societies, we are further away from plausible solutions than when the digital revolution began.

Unlike the Industrial Revolution, it is taking place in a hyper-democratic world. Peter Thiel was right, of course; Twitter cannot be compared to the invention of printing, or flying cars. Yet he was also wrong. We live in a world where everyone with a grievance wields more digital power in the palm of their hand than the computers that sent Apollo 14 into orbit. The Industrial Revolution was unleashed on undemocratic – or in the case of Britain and the US, semi-democratic – societies. Moreover, it made economic sense for Victorian elites to buy social peace by broadening the electoral franchise. What price are our elites prepared to pay this time round?

Given how quickly the digital economy is spreading, the sooner our politics wakes up to the challenge the better. 'Go west, young man' was the best career advice in the nineteenth century. Today's equivalent is probably 'get an engineering degree', but it will not necessarily be as lucrative. A third of Americans who graduated in STEM subjects (science, technology, engineering and maths) are in jobs that do not require any such qualification.[52] They must still pay off their student debts. Up and down America there are programmers working as office temps and even fast-food servers. In the age of artificial intelligence, more and more will drift into obsolescence. On the evidence so far, this latest technological revolution is different in its dynamics from earlier ones. In contrast to earlier disruptions, which affected particular sectors of the economy, the effects of today's revolution are general-purpose. From janitors to surgeons, virtually no jobs will be immune. Whether you are training to be an airline pilot, a retail assistant, a lawyer or a financial trader, labour-saving technology is whittling down your numbers – in some cases drastically so. In 2000, financial services employed 150,000 people in New York. By 2013 that had dropped to 100,000. Over the same period, Wall Street's profits have soared. Up to 70 per cent of all equity trades are now executed by algorithms.[53]

Or take social media. In 2006, Google bought YouTube for $1.65 billion. It had sixty-five employees, so the price amounted to $25 million per employee. In 2012 Facebook bought Instagram, which had thirteen employees, for $1 billion. That came to $77 million per employee. In 2014, it bought WhatsApp, with fifty-five employees, for $19 billion, at a staggering $345 million per employee.[54] Such riches are little comfort to the thousands of engineers who cannot find work. Facebook's data servers are now managed by Cyborg, a software program. It requires one human technician for every twenty thousand computers. Almost any job that involves sitting in front of a screen and manipulating information is disappearing, or will do soon. Software can now drive cars and mark student essays. By skewing the gains of the new economy to a few, robots also weaken the chief engine of growth: middle-class demand. As labour becomes pricier relative to machines, spending power falls. The US economy produces more than a third more today than it did in 1998 with the same-sized labour force and a significantly larger population. It still makes sense for people to obtain degrees. Graduates earn more than those who have completed only high school. But their returns are falling. The median pay for US entry-level graduates fell from $52,000 in 2000 to $46,000 in 2014.[55] It was flat for postgraduates. Higher education is by no means a catch-all solution. Not every kid is a frustrated Einstein. Some are better suited to skilled trades.

Technology is often treated as a separate force to globalisation. In reality they are the same thing. The first great phase of globalisation, which went up in flames in the First World War, was driven by steam power. It would have been uneconomic to ship Asian goods to Europe under sail, or to send the finished products back that way. They would have corrupted or taken too long to turn a profit. Before steam, inter-continental trade was limited to a trickle of non-perishable cargo, such as silk, spices and slaves (a high share of the West's human cargo from Africa did die en route, but the ratio of survivors still made such ventures tragically profitable). Steam changed all that, and the revolution came much quicker than we might think. In 1825 Britain had around four thousand wooden ships and zero steam ships. By 1860 it commanded 389,000 tonnes of iron steam.[56] Britain's maritime tonnage jumped a hundredfold in less than two generations. It is no accident that the Opium Wars began in the midst of the steam revolution. The pressure for free trade with China was boosted by the ease with which it could now be done. Nor is it a coincidence that Indian raw textile exports took off in the 1860s, just as America's slave-owning south was closed off by the Civil War. It was only after the advent of steam that Britain turned decisively against the slave trade. Industrialisation made slave ownership uneconomic. What could be achieved using free labour rather than human chattels was far more efficient with cotton-picking machines. Steam power clinched the deal. It also transformed politics and diplomacy. It took Thomas Jefferson two weeks to travel from Philadelphia, America's then capital, to his estate in Monticello at the turn of the nineteenth century. By 1850, the same journey could be done by steam train in one day.[57] The human story is written in tears, as they say (and joy, it should be added). They are right. It is also measured in technology.

Who is to say our disruption will end up any different? Though the wrench was painful, the Industrial Revolution eventually lifted everyone's standard of living in the West – and now that of billions of people across the world. But the debate that is raging over the future of technology is nowhere near reaching a consensus. Some economists believe the future impact of robots, and artificial intelligence, has been greatly exaggerated. If they are right, that would be great news for the legions of truck, delivery, cab and Uber drivers who earn their living from driving vehicles. It would also be a relief for the future of our politics. If you include those who work part-time, there are more Americans and British working behind the wheel today than employed in manufacturing jobs.[58] The numbers for continental

Europe vary considerably – a higher share of Germans, for example, still work in manufacturing. But the impact on Germany of the emergence of self-driving vehicles would still be dramatic. Wherever you look, the large majority of drivers are male. Though I try to avoid generalising about gender, it is fair to say that men are less adaptable to disruptions in their work routines than women, and more liable to vent their anger politically. To anyone who doubts that, I have a flying car to sell you. Meanwhile, remind yourselves of the impact manufacturing job losses have had on Western politics. Way more than half of Trump's voters were male. The same applies to the Brexit electorate.

As the baseball legend Yogi Berra allegedly said, it is tough to make predictions – especially about the future. The economist Robert Gordon clearly wasn't listening. His book *The Rise and Fall of American Growth* makes a startling forecast that did not go down well in Silicon Valley. The future is not what it used to be, he says. The peak age of high growth and disruptive technology is behind us. Forget the power of the iPhone. Stop exulting about Google's driverless car. Such wonders pale beside the changes felt by earlier generations. They are unlikely to be matched by our age. Gordon's thesis is not entirely new. Tyler Cowen made a similar argument with his sparkling monograph *The Great Stagnation* (ironically first published as an ebook). Nor is it as counterintuitive as it sounds to our app-crowded, WiFi-saturated twenty-first-century brains. Gordon points out that for most of history, growth was absent. Between the fall of the Roman Empire and the Middle Ages there was basically none. England's per-capita income doubled between 1300 and 1700, a rate so slow as to be imperceptible.[59] Life for most people was unimaginably stunted. Only in the nineteenth century did that change.

Fast growth, in other words, is a recent blip, not a constant. For China, India and others, today's high growth is an historical transition that will also plateau. Picture the typical American household in 1870 (or indeed much of Africa and India today). It was rural, and often isolated. Almost one in four of its children could be expected to die in infancy. The rest would live to fifty if they were lucky. They would spend much of their lives fetching water from wells, gathering wood for the stove, making clothes out of crude cloth and suffering from whatever incurable diseases struck them. Travel was by horse for the most part. A quarter of all US agricultural land, worked by no fewer than 8.6 million labourers, was given over to producing horse feed.[60] Communication was by letter for those who could read. Light came from whale oil or kerosene. '[The] fruits of their labor were at the mercy of droughts, floods, and infestations of insects,' says Gordon. There was little, in other words, to mark out the squalor of daily lives from countless generations before. Then came the great leap forward. Commercial electricity, the internal combustion engine, penicillin, synthetics, refrigeration and the telephone – to name just a few of the new wonders – turned life inside out. Land was freed up to produce food for humans. The stench of horse manure was cleared from the streets. Piped water and gas entered the home. Thomas Edison paved the way for the skyscraper with electric lifts. By 1950 only one in a hundred American children died in infancy. The rest could expect to live to seventy or beyond.[61] By then, almost all of them were literate. Journeys were reduced from weeks to hours. Within the blink of a historical eye, life went from nasty, brutish and short to pleasant, bright and relatively lengthy. For those who still believe our age's disruptions match what happened after 1870, ask yourself which you would first give up, your iPhone or the flush toilet? Laptop or antibiotics? If you have trouble answering those, ponder life without electricity. It is a measure of our solipsism that we take for granted what went before.[62]

Between 1870 and 1970 – the century of the West's greatest productivity growth – incomes grew far faster than ever experienced. They also exceeded anything we in the West have seen since. With the exception of the 1990s, when the digital revolution hit our desktops, productivity growth has slowed sharply in the past half-century. In America it dropped from an average of 2.7 per cent a year in the 1950s and 1960s to below 1 per cent in the last decade. As a result, income growth has also slowed. The median US household income in 2014 was $50,600. If we had maintained pre-1970 productivity growth, it would have been $97,300.[63] We are already well into a slowdown that, in Gordon's view, is likely to slow further. This is where his thesis becomes controversial. According to the optimists, such as Erik Brynjolfsson and Andrew McAfee, the future is accelerating and will generally bring happy results. Their book, *The Second Machine Age*, argues that intensifying automation will free up labour for more interesting pursuits – and leisure. Theirs is a vision of abundance.

I recently heard a well-known Silicon Valley investor dismiss the doubters as ignoramuses. He pointed to the efflorescence of tech unicorns – private start-ups valued at more than $1 billion – that are working on virtual reality, artificial intelligence, gene-splicing medicine and the like. At least one will be as transformative as the iPhone, he said. In fact, the pessimists' gloom makes ample room for the emergence of virtual headsets, driverless cars and robotic disruptions. The impact of new technologies will be significant but not game-changing, they say. Today's medical progress is only adding to economic stagnation. Most recent advances are in the treatment of physical ailments, thus prolonging life for those who can afford them. There have been no comparable breakthroughs in curing mental illness, such as Alzheimer's. Longer lives at the same rates of mental incapacity will be bad for productivity. Technology may continue to surprise in dazzling ways. But if the iPhone did not lift productivity rates, what could? Perhaps 3D printing? Or a cryonic leap into immortality?

Initially, I feared Gordon's pessimism was correct. Silicon Valley's wilder futurologists make it easy to dismiss the future as bunk. Now my fear is that Gordon is wrong. We should be careful what we wish for. It looks increasingly likely we are going to get it. Again, to grasp this, think about the world as a whole. What has befallen the West's blue-collar workforce in the last generation is the shift of routine physical tasks to the factory floors of the developing world. This was enabled by the relentless drop in the cost of transport. What steam did in the nineteenth century, aeroplanes, supertankers and mechanised ports did for the last third of the twentieth century. The explosion of communications technology in the twenty-first century is enabling Western companies to do precisely the same in the knowledge economy today. Companies' ability to go offshore via diversified global supply chains is no longer confined to physical goods. In the short term it is not artificial intelligence the West should worry about. It is what Baldwin calls remote intelligence. In some respects it has already arrived. Over the last twenty years, India and the Philippines reaped the rewards of the telecoms revolution to create lower-skilled service sector jobs at call centres, and on technology helpdesks. Those jobs are now under threat. As the venture capitalist Marc Andreessen says, 'Software is eating the world'. How many times have you talked to a computer recently, rather than someone with an Indian accent? A lot more than a few years ago, I would guess. Automated voice software is supplanting humans. India is thus being forced to upgrade. Its next generation of offshore jobs will be devoted to far more complex tasks, such as providing medical diagnoses, writing legal briefs, remotely supervising factories and plants, and doing consumer data analysis. In fact, it is already happening.

The speed with which virtual presence and holographic telepresence are improving is opening up whole areas. So too are rapid leaps in language-translation software (India should beware: China's relative lack of English will no longer be such a disadvantage). In the West we spend half our time fretting about low-skilled immigrants. We should be worrying at least as much about high-skilled offshoring. Some types of medical surgeon and architect will be as vulnerable to remote intelligence as plant engineers or call-centre operators. Ironically, some of the lowest-paid jobs – in barbershops and nail salons – will be among the safest. No matter how dexterous your virtual service provider, it is hard to imagine how she could cut your hair. In the near future, technology will shift many more lucrative Western service jobs to the developing world. Beyond that, artificial intelligence threatens to eat the whole world's lunch. China's factory jobs are already ceding ground to the robots. Likewise, every country's service sector will eventually come into play – starting with the West, where the game is well under way.

The big question is: how far will it go? Much further than we think. Between a fifth and a third of the Western labour force is already engaged in independent work, the McKinsey Global Institute estimates, which it defines as 'short-term, piece rate and autonomous'. Society's move towards self-employment is still in its infancy yet it already totals 162 million people.[64] These are either fully self-employed, or supplementing full-time jobs with part-time work. A growing share of such work is done online, or found online. Roughly a third are free agents doing independent work because they want to, such as web designers or artists working for themselves. These are the last people we need worry about. Indeed, many of us might envy their freedom. But a third are full-time independents because they are financially strapped. In other words, there are already about 50 million Westerners trying to earn their living in the gig economy out of necessity rather than choice. France and Spain have the highest share of independent workers, with almost a third of their labour force doing so either full- or part-time. The US and Britain are somewhat lower, at just over a quarter. The largest platforms are household names, such as Uber, with 1 million drivers, Freelancer.com with 18 million users and Airbnb with 2.5 million listings. Smaller ones include Task Rabbit, where people are available to do odd jobs of all kinds, and Hourly Nerd, which temps out software and finance professionals to organise your digital files or do your taxes. Not all are in financial straits. Some people get a nice boost renting out their apartments online, without the bureaucratic headache of setting up a bed and breakfast.

But a rising share has been forced by low pay or redundancy into the informal jobs market. They account for *all* of jobs growth since the Great Recession. In the US, formal employment has shrunk by 0.1 per cent a year since the 2008 financial meltdown. All of America's new jobs have been generated by independent work, which has risen by 7.8 per cent a year.[65] The next time an economist boasts about America's low unemployment rate, remember that number means something very different from what it used to. This is not your parents' economy. It is not even your older sister's. Nor is the gig economy dominated by millennials. Britain has more pensioners doing independent work than people under thirty. In America, the labour force participation rate for people aged between sixty-four and seventy-five has jumped by 4.7 per cent in the last decade, a time when the overall rate has dropped.[66] We like to call it the sharing economy. But the fact that older people are doing such a large share of the work suggests a less charitable force is at play. As the real value of pensions and social security goes down, the pressure to postpone retirement grows. Again, we should be careful not to generalise: some older people are working because they enjoy it. Yet we should not romanticise what is happening either. The age of automation is making labour increasingly dispensable, so companies are constantly on the lookout for ways to slim down. The new economy has created digital platforms that enable people to offer their services online. Yet what they find is generally far less secure than what they lost. Such work does not provide healthcare or matching retirement contributions. Nor does it always pay. Almost three-quarters of independent workers in the US report serious difficulties in chasing up what they are owed. Average arrears were $6000 – a large sum for those on the edge. Almost half of Americans would be unable to pay a $400 medical emergency bill without going into debt.[67] What McKinsey forecasts for the future of independent work is both revealing and disturbing. By their estimates, each Western household could save an average of 3.2 hours a day by outsourcing work online to odd-jobbers: driving the children to school, running errands, doing the shopping, cooking, laundry and looking after the pets. In total, this would create seven million new jobs. McKinsey calculates that there is $100 billion of unpaid household work that should be outsourced, which would take up twelve billion hours of work time. It takes two seconds to figure out this would pay just over $8 an hour – considerably below the minimum wage in most of the West. Such a shift would be great for those who could afford it. But it is hardly an inspiring vision of the future of digital-enabled work.

We often kid ourselves that the disruptive economy is driven by creativity. But most of it involves the extreme application of digital networks to whatever area applies. Our dreams of the future are supplied by cyber-utopians. But for most people the reality today is less glamorous. Reporters are losing jobs to algorithmic content farms that write news reports based on keywords that push them to the top of the Google search page. Advertising representatives are being made redundant by mobile social media advertisements that know exactly where you are and will match their pitch to your location. Facebook is now able to use your friends' faces in ads aimed specifically at you. Jaron Lanier, a pioneer of virtual technology, yet one of the most grounded voices in Silicon Valley, calls the big firms that are cornering the consumer data market the 'siren servers' – after the creatures of Greek myth.[68] The rest of us are sailors being lured onto the rocks. In exchange for access to social media, we surrender more and more of our personal data for free.

The exchange is increasingly one-sided. Many of our jobs are squeezed by this invisible bargain – and if not our jobs, then our earnings, which never seem to rise. The result is to shrink the worth of the real economy by reducing most consumers' ability to pay. Even for the owners of the siren servers, this will ultimately prove self-defeating: 'The dominant principle of the new economy, the information economy, has lately been to conceal the value of information, of all things,' Lanier says. 'Ordinary people will be unvalued ... while those closest to the top computers will become hypervaluable.' After a while, the data elites may too feel the pinch. Their business model is the opposite of what Henry Ford did when he raised the wage he paid to factory employees to $5 a day, a sum that in the 1920s would afford a comfortable middle-class lifestyle. Three decades later, Ford switched his model when he began to invest in automation. On a tour of the plant with Walter Reuther, the auto union leader, Ford pointed at the robots and said: 'How will you get union dues from them?' Reuther replied: 'How will you get them to buy your cars?'[69] It was a good question. We might ask the same today of Google or Facebook. The new economy requires consumers with spending power – just as the old one did. Yet much like the farmer who eats his seed corn, Big Data is gobbling up its source of future revenue. 'It's not a result of some evil scheme,' writes Lanier, 'but a side effect of an idiotic elevation of the fantasy that technology is getting smart and standing on its own without people.'

Whether you listen to utopians or dystopians, all agree the share of jobs at risk of elimination is rising. McKinsey says almost half of existing jobs are vulnerable to robots. We are ill-equipped to adapt. Two-thirds of children entering school today will end up in types of job that currently do not exist. Nobody has yet found a remedy. Europe and America's populist right wants to turn the clock back to the days when men were men and the West ruled. It is prepared to sacrifice the gains of globalisation – and risk conflict with China – to protect jobs that have already vanished. Populists have little to say about automation, though it is a far larger threat to people's jobs than trade. The left urges incremental steps such as better worker training, smarter schools and infrastructure. These are worthy causes. But they are a bit like prescribing aspirin for cancer. Before her ill-fated run for the presidency, Hillary Clinton was asked about rising structural unemployment: 'I don't have a quick glib answer for you. There are no easy fixes.' Even the non-populist right has thrown up its hands. In its study of the future of work, the laissez-faire Baker Institute admitted it had been 'unable to find any solutions based on the free market'. Karl Marx predicted that capitalism would push the workers of the world to unite. He got it back to front. It is the elites who are loosening their allegiances and workers who are reaching for national flags. This is hardly a vision of social peace. 'The rich will live in gated communities, and secure compounds, that are protected by drones and connected by driverless cars,' predict Yascha Mounk and Lee Drutman, two of the sharpest political scientists around. 'Ever smarter surveillance technologies will help to monitor the activities of the malcontents outside . . .'[70] Elites of the world unite! You have everything to lose.

———

Every January, the Davos gathering sounds a little more bemused about what is happening in the world outside. In 2016 it worried about the threat of mass disease, just as the Ebola epidemic was receding. In 2015, its annual report dwelt on the return of geopolitics following Russia's annexation of Crimea the year before.[71] In its first report in 2006 it was anxious about epidemics and the risk of terrorism after the Asian flu crisis and the London Underground attacks. And so on. Davos specialises in projecting the future from a recent past that took it by surprise.

We are all guilty of this. But Davos has made a brand of its blow-dried conventional wisdom. George Orwell said that 'the great enemy of clear language is insincerity'. By that measure the global elites have something to hide – although I believe they are concealing it mainly from themselves. The more our elites call for 'thought leadership' and 'disruptive thinking', the less they seem to mean it. Buzz terms, such as resiliency, global governance, multi-stakeholder collaboration and digital public square, are the answer to every problem, regardless of its nature. Too many wars happening? We need more collaboration. High risk of another global pandemic? More stakeholder participation. Populist revolts convulsing the Western world? We must rebuild trust in global governance.

For every risk, Davos offers an identikit fix. Most of its Latinate prose sounds innocuous. But the lexicon betrays a worldview that is inherently wary of public opinion. Democracy is never a cure. If the middle classes are angry, they should listen more closely. Here was Davos's 2015 solution to economic populism: 'Without trust, no decisions at the international level will be taken. However, the responsibility extends beyond the political level: multinational companies and consumers also have a role to play to strengthen the argument in favour of global collaboration in the face of growing pressures to prioritize national economic self-interest.'[72] Translation: Democracies must listen more to multinational companies. Pursuing national economic self-interest is always a bad thing. Here is Davos's solution to multipolar disorder: 'Managing this risk will require flexibility, fresh thinking and multistakeholder communication.' No translation required – though it would be good to get a preview of the fresh thinking that Davos keeps saying we need.

The gulf between the view from the Swiss Alps and realities on the ground continually widens. Given the electoral shocks of the previous year, the 2017 outlook is the best example to date. This is Davos's solution to the immigration crisis convulsing European and American politics: 'To some extent, the cultural challenges associated with immigration could be tackled by getting better at communicating change: data show that voters will change their views on cultural changes in society if politicians highlight the assimilation already taking place.'[73] Which means that we need to get better at telling people how well things are going. And here is its cure for the West's crisis of democracy: 'One potential solution could be to make better use of technology in the process of government – not only to deliver services in a faster, more transparent, inclusive and consumer-oriented way, but also to establish a "digital public square" with more direct communication between leaders and people.'[74] Politicians should thus spend more time online. Davos perhaps ought first to have read what people are saying on the internet. As one person quipped about Donald Trump's Twitter-propelled candidacy, 'It is like the comments section running for president.' If this is thought leadership, how does thought followership sound?

Davos has become the emblem of a global elite that has lost its ability to listen.

I began this book with a reminiscence about the fall of the Berlin Wall. A decade later, I found myself employed as speechwriter to Lawrence Summers, when he was the US Secretary of the Treasury in the Clinton administration. Looking back, I am astonished at that era's unshakeable self-confidence. This was the high noon of the Washington Consensus. Alongside Alan Greenspan, the chairman of the US Federal Reserve, and Robert Rubin, the previous Treasury Secretary, Summers personified the global intellectual elite. Though often abrasive, he is also brilliant – especially when he is wrong. But when the facts change he is capable of changing his mind. By 2008 he had already walked away from much of the triumphalism of the late 1990s. Summers complained of 'the development of stateless elites whose allegiance is to global economic success and their own prosperity rather than the interests of the nation where they are headquartered'.[75] By 2016, he was warning that the public's tolerance for expert solutions 'appears to have been exhausted'. He advised a new 'responsible nationalism', which would 'begin from the idea that the basic responsibility of government is to maximize the welfare of its citizens, not to pursue some abstract concept of the global good'.[76] The global elites, in other words, need to catch up with how most people view the world – not the other way round. I believe what Summers is saying now is closer to the truth.

According to the World Values Survey, people identify far more strongly with their nation than with a global identity. The two exceptions were Colombia, which has been racked by a brutal civil war for more than a generation, and Andorra, which has fewer than eighty thousand people. The more we cede power to global bodies, the more virulent the backlash against globalisation. Dani Rodrik, one of the world's leading international economists, talks of the global trilemma.[77] We cannot simultaneously pursue democracy, national determination and economic globalisation. They are incompatible. One of them has to go. Under the old General Agreement on Tariffs and Trade (GATT), which ended in 1995, any nation was free to veto any deal. Nowadays democracies routinely suffer reversals in the WTO's appellate court. For example, the European Union's objections to importing genetically modified foods and hormone-infused beef were overruled by the WTO even though it conceded the science was unsettled. If the democratically backed will of the world's largest trading bloc can be undone by a group of unelected trade judges, imagine the odds for anyone else.

The space for national democracy is shrinking. Vast areas that were once the preserve of national sovereignty are now ring-fenced by international law and global regulation. The instinct in Davos is to push even more policy-making out of the range of nation states. The answer to Europe's problems is always more Europe. The answer to the global trade backlash is always to sell trade deals more effectively. It should come as no surprise that democracies are now loath to ratify such agreements. The last time any serious world trade talks were held in a Western city was in Seattle in 1999. It was shut down by protesters. The next time global leaders made the attempt was in 2002, from the safe space of the Arabian Gulf where no dissenters could be heard. The Doha Round died a few years later. Now Donald Trump has killed the Trans-Pacific Partnership, the deal that was launched by George W. Bush and completed by Barack Obama. Trump is also picking apart the Clinton-era North American Free Trade Agreement and has buried hopes of a transatlantic agreement. Britain, meanwhile, is abandoning the European single market.

The world's elites have helped to provoke what they feared: a populist uprising against the world economy. Globalisation is going into reverse just as the impact of new technology is showing signs of picking up. In his Harvard class, Rodrik offers students a choice: Should we globalise democracy, or restrict it at home? Students always vote strongly for global democracy. But if it does not work at the European level, what chance would it stand worldwide? Digital democracy, meanwhile, is an empty slogan. The other choice – autocracy – is a bleak prospect, though a disturbingly broad range of nations are edging towards it. Which leaves us with one practical alternative: abandoning the drive to deep globalisation. Rodrik calls this 'thin globalisation'. I prefer to think of it as the last chance for liberal democracy. It may be the only realistic way of salvaging a peaceful global order. In the 1990s, Thomas Friedman, the *New York Times* columnist, came up with his famous Golden Straitjacket for the brave new world that came after the fall of the Berlin Wall.[78] Ironically, this meant less democracy precisely at the moment of its triumph. When you put on the Golden Straitjacket, 'your economy grows and your politics shrinks'. Friedman possesses an uncanny knack for catching the spirit of the age with revealing insights. But he should have dropped the word golden. Straitjackets are for lunatics. We can hardly complain if our democracies have begun to lose their minds.

PART TWO

REACTION

Democracy is not the multiplication of ignorant opinions.

BEATRICE WEBB

S uccess breeds imitation. Until I was six years old, there were
barely thirty democracies in a world of almost two hundred
nations. The first wave of modern democratisation happened in
1974, when Portugal's Carnation Revolution toppled Salazar's
fascist regime in Lisbon.[1] It was followed swiftly by the overthrow of the military junta in Greece. More or less the same
happened in Spain the following year, after the death of General
Franco. These closed the accounts on fascism's defeat a generation earlier. It was not until the fall of the Berlin Wall that the
floodgates really opened. By the turn of the millennium there
were more than a hundred democracies worldwide. Just as the
Washington Consensus provided the toolkit for economic success, so the West supplied the user manual on how to democra-
tise. They were companion volumes: you could not develop your
economy unless you were a democracy, or so we claimed. The

two also shared an unapologetic ignorance of history, which meant they were seriously misleading. In reality, economies have often developed behind protectionist walls – that is what almost every Western country did in the nineteenth century. Had we forgotten that Alexander Hamilton's 'infant industry' protections carried through into the twentieth century? Hamilton took this mercantilist approach directly from England's Tudor monarchs, who used protections to shield English wool manufacturers from their Flemish competitors. Likewise, plenty of countries have industrialised under authoritarian conditions. Otto von Bismarck took Germany on the blood and iron road to prosperity in the late nineteenth century. Japan's Meiji Restoration was a paragon of top-down development. What about China over the last generation – and today? But the West was on a proselytising mission. The big questions had been settled. These were minor potholes on our teleological journey.

Things started to go wrong after 2000. The first great blow was in Russia, where Vladimir Putin replaced Boris Yeltsin as president and set about closing down the system of free and fair elections while retaining its trappings. The West is good at screening out local detail when it is inconvenient, particularly in regard to Russia. In the 1980s, the Soviet Union's collapse humiliated an entire generation of Western Sovietologists. None had been expecting it. In the 1990s, we convinced ourselves Russia was in transition from socialist autocracy to liberal capitalism, even while Western consultants urged Moscow to adopt shock therapy, which would enable the rise of a new Russian oligarchy. On Western advice, Yeltsin privatised Russia's most valuable state assets in a fire sale to a small coterie of business-men in exchange for bankrolling his 1996 re-election. Still our faith was unshaken. In 2008, we believed Putin's authoritarian interregnum had ended and that Russia had resumed its journey to sunlit uplands under Dimitry Medvedev. The Obama admin-istration based its reset of US–Russia relations on the belief that Putin was a has-been. It was a bet that proved far costlier than Obama and the then Secretary of State Hillary Clinton could have imagined. When I visited Moscow two weeks after Donald Trump's election in 2016, my hosts were crowing that America had just experienced its own colour revolution. From Georgia's Rose Revolution in 2003 to Ukraine's Orange Revo-lution the following year, and Moldova's Grape version in 2009, we had cheered the fall of pro-Moscow regimes along Russia's borders. Trump's victory revealed that two could play that game. Suddenly everything solid was melting into air. In place of the march towards truth, we had reality-TV politics. 'Moscow can feel like an oligarchy in the morning and a democracy in the afternoon, a monarchy for dinner and a totalitarian state by bedtime,' wrote Peter Pomerantsev, in his book *Nothing Is True and Everything Is Possible*.[2] Such manipulations are starting to feel ominously familiar in Trump's America.

Democracy's brand was also damaged by America's reaction to the Al Qaeda attacks in 2001. George W. Bush's response to

9/11 dealt a twin blow to Western democracy's allure. The first came in the form of the Patriot Act, which paved the way for spying on American citizens and gave the green light to multiple dilutions of US constitutional liberties. That imperative was then extended to America's relations with any country, democratic or not, which pledged to cooperate in the 'war on terror'. Autocrats such as Putin and Pakistan's Pervez Musharraf went from pariahs to soul brothers almost overnight. When the Bush administration said 'You are either with us or against us,' it was referring to the opening of 'black sites' where the CIA could waterboard terrorist suspects, and the no-questions-asked exchanges of terrorist lists against which there was little prospect of appeal – a practice known in international law as *refoulement*. This gave undemocratic regimes an excuse to logroll domestic opponents onto the international lists, with devastating effects on political rights around the world. In the decade after 9/11, the number of Interpol red notices rose eightfold.[3] Such practices belied Bush's democratic agenda. For example, it robbed the US of the moral standing to criticise the Shanghai Cooperation Organization, a China-backed body of central Asian autocracies that today operates its own *refoulement* exchanges of political dissidents in the name of counter-terrorism. The Bush administration's approach was also geopolitically shortsighted. Just as the West's support for the Afghan jihad against the Soviets in the 1980s laid the ground for the rise of Islamist terrorism, so America's Faustian post-9/11 pacts with autocratic regimes helped sow the seeds for the world's current democratic recession. That is certain to deepen under Trump.

But the 'war on terror' was the lesser of Bush's unintended consequences. The bigger one came in March 2003 with the US-led invasion of Iraq. It is hard to overstate the damage the Iraq War did to America's global soft power – and to the credibility of the West's democratic mission. Operation Enduring Freedom, which began after 9/11, was followed by Operation Iraqi Freedom. Both were rashly named. It is one thing to go to war in the name of liberty; quite another to be clueless about it. Even without the doublespeak of the 'war on terror', it is highly questionable whether democracy can be installed from the barrel of a gun. Much of the exemplary work America had done to promote civic exchanges and facilitate dissent behind the Iron Curtain during the Cold War was undone by the cavalier way in which Bush's Coalition Provisional Authority set about democratising Iraq. Washington flooded Baghdad with a bunch of twenty- and thirty-something political hacks who were given colonial-type powers to set policy in Iraq's unformed democracy. The PR fallout from the Bush appointees' ignorance of local conditions was compounded by horrific images of the humiliations US national guards meted out to prisoners in Abu Ghraib. Operation Iraqi Freedom had turned into Operation Damage Democracy.

It was the desire to avoid repeating Bush's blunders that

caused Barack Obama such indecision when the Arab Spring erupted in 2011. At first Obama supported the pro-democracy protests in Cairo's Tahrir Square and beyond. When he saw the results – most notably in the profoundly illiberal rule of the Muslim Brotherhood in Egypt – he went cold on the revolutions. One by one the Arab democratic flowers withered. Only in Tunisia is democracy still alive. Obama's ambivalence was perhaps best expressed in his administration's little-noticed annual budget requests for the National Endowment for Democracy, a US body that has carried out patient work in helping young democracies to take root. In each of the five years after the Arab Spring, the White House asked for a reduction in the NED's budget.[4] Against all the trends, the Republican Congress reversed Obama's cuts and increased its allocation. By this stage Obama was hopelessly conflicted. On a 2015 trip to Ethiopia, he congratulated its government on being democratically elected following a general election in which the ruling party had taken every single seat. Shortly afterwards Addis Ababa launched a crackdown on its opponents that resulted in hundreds of deaths. If America's president was in two minds about democracy, how was the rest of the world supposed to feel? It was on Obama's watch that the tally of global democracies fell most sharply. The world now has twenty-five fewer democracies than it did at the turn of the century. In addition to Russia and Venezuela, Turkey, Thailand, Botswana and now Hungary are deemed to have crossed the threshold. According to Freedom House, more countries have restricted than expanded freedom every year since 2008.[5] 'There is not a single country on the African continent where democracy is firmly consolidated and secure,' says Larry Diamond, one of the leading scholars of democracy.[6] What we do not yet know is whether the world's democratic recession will turn into a global depression. Fukuyama's question will be answered largely within the West itself.

The seesaw effects of US foreign policy since 2000 were of a second order compared to the Great Recession's impact on the West's democratic reputation. Whether you blamed the crash on greedy investment bankers or the incompetence of financial regulators largely depended on your politics. But in both cases, from a Western perspective the 2008 meltdown was first and foremost an economic event. The rest of the world, however, regarded 2008 and its aftermath through a much wider aperture. Although the short-term market turmoil was worldwide, the so-called global recession was primarily an Atlantic one. Most of the rest of the world continued to expand. Indeed, growth in China, the world's largest autocracy, picked up for several years after 2008. The contrast did wonders for China's global image. It was also a boon to its political reputation. Although the West likes to think of the late twentieth-century democratic wave as a Damascene conversion, much of it was purely instrumental: non-Westerners could observe the fruits of Western growth on their television screens. They knew which goose was laying the golden eggs. Once China's economy visibly decoupled from the

West in 2008, the tide began to turn. 'By demonstrating that advanced modernization can be combined with authoritarian rule, the Chinese regime has given hope to authoritarian rulers everywhere,' says Andrew Nathan, a leading Sinologist.[7]

China put its newfound prestige to work on multiple fronts. The most widely felt has been economic. China's development banks pumped billions of dollars into Africa, Central Asia and Latin America – often displacing Western-dominated global institutions, such as the World Bank, and the Asian Development Bank. In contrast to its Bretton Woods competitors, China's lenders offered loans without attaching pro-democracy strings. In 2015 it launched the Beijing-based Asian Infrastructure Investment Bank. The Obama White House publicly urged its allies to boycott this new body. This was ignored.[8] Britain, France, Germany, Australia and others joined the AIIB as founding shareholders. Likewise, China stepped up spending on soft power. Beijing now runs more than five hundred Confucius Institutes worldwide.[9] At a time when Western media outlets are on the global retreat – in some cases shutting down any foreign presence – China Central Television (CCTV) has set up thirty new overseas bureaus. Others are following suit. RT, Russia's state-backed television channel, is now viewed in three million hotel rooms across the world.

China does not share the West's missionary impulse – it no longer seeks to export revolution, as it did during the days of Chairman Mao. Its goal nowadays is primarily counter-revolutionary: like Moscow, Beijing's real aim is to rupture the West's claims to universalism. Given the latter's dubious record in Iraq and elsewhere, this is not a hard sell. It is easier than before to make the case that America's liberal-democratic discourse is a cover for its geopolitical interests. China's mantra of respect for civilisational diversity – a code term for autocracy – now finds more receptive audiences. Dirigisme has earned a second look. One of the most insidious trends, yet one of the least remarked upon, is the spread of restrictions on foreign non-governmental organisations. Led by China and Russia, almost forty countries have muzzled, or expelled, foreign NGOs since 2003 – most of them Western.[10] Some of this is pure repression: a number of China's allies in Central Asia have used the pretext of 'homosexual propaganda' to deny entry to foreign charities. Elsewhere, the backlash is more subtle. Much as RT and CCTV keep up the pretence of editorial independence, so authoritarian regimes have acquired the habit of setting up government-backed NGOs – the oxymoronic Gongos (government-organised non-governmental organisations). Gongos are another Chinese speciality. As I say, success breeds imitation.

Then there is Donald Trump. How could the world's wealthiest democracy put such a man in its top job? It is a question that has deeply puzzled China. The Communist Party's traditional view on US democracy is that America's moneyed classes engineer the victory of the candidate who can best defend the interests of capital. The process is always a sham. The view of

China's pro-democracy groups, on the other hand, is that the American people freely choose the best person after a vigorous and fair debate. Both schools have been turned inside out by the 2016 outcome: China's conservatives because Trump won against the wishes of Wall Street, which is not meant to happen in a capitalist democracy; China's liberals because charlatans like Trump are not supposed to win. The process should be foolproof. 'China's liberals are in a bind,' says Eric Li, a Chinese venture capitalist in Shanghai, who runs his own thinktank. 'They despise Trump. But they can't quite bring themselves to say . . . the people are wrong. Such an admission would not help them make the case for Western-style democracy in China. After all, if the people can be so wrong, how can you give them the vote?'[11]

From America's post-9/11 blunders to Donald Trump's election, the twenty-first century has been generous to autocrats everywhere. It is tempting to believe these were historic accidents that will iron themselves out in due course. The human, social and technological forces favouring democracy will ultimately prove far stronger than the 'shit happens' school of history. It is a train of thought we should avoid. Bertolt Brecht, the great German playwright, famously said: 'Would it not be easier / In that case for the government / To dissolve the people / And elect another?' In a strange way that is what Putin does by manipulating and remaking Russian public opinion to suit his purposes. Messing with people's heads is also Trump's specialty.

It is harder to manufacture consent – or bottle up dissent – in America than anywhere else in the world. But that does not make it impossible. Democracy, like society, is an adaptive organism. In one form or another, most Western democracies have long enshrined the people as sovereign (Britain is one of the exceptions that prove the rule). Yet we have always known there is no such thing as the people. It is a useful fiction. Perhaps the curtain has now been pulled too far back for us to keep up the pretence. In another flight of wit, Brecht once said: 'All power comes from the people. But where does it go?'[12]

––––––––––

In my gut, I did not expect Donald Trump to win. However bad things had become, when the hour arrived the American electorate would step back from the abyss. I was wrong about that. I was closer to the mark about his competition. Long before Trump came on the scene, it was obvious Hillary Clinton could only win the presidency by default. Regardless of how awful her opponent might be, a grudging victory was the best she could hope for. Her tone-deafness towards the middle class was almost serene. The same was true of much of the tentacular universe of consultants, politicos, alumni and friends who constituted Hillaryland. Such was their faith in America's demographic currents that they rarely doubted that Clinton's rainbow coalition would carry her over the line. History was on their side.

(A similar sense of destiny blinded many British fans of the European Union in the lead-up to the Brexit vote.) One otherwise insightful friend, who was expecting to play a role in a Clinton administration, insisted to me that it was mathematically impossible for a Republican to win the White House. Even if the white middle classes despised Hillary, they would still be outnumbered. If demography was destiny, why waste energy on new thinking? 'All that Hillary Clinton need do – or whoever takes the Democratic nomination – is tick the right boxes and let demography fix the rest,' I wrote in 2014.[13] 'Such is the US left's worldview. It is also a measure of its intellectual poverty. Whatever liberals are smoking, it is no stimulant to new ideas.' But Mrs Clinton had put her trust in the numbers. At the core of her electoral machine were the data gurus. 'Everyday Americans', as Mrs Clinton called the middle classes, were simply props. I have spent a fair amount of time interviewing leaders of ultra-nationalist movements, cult groups and fanatics of all kinds around the world. I have yet to come across a more airtight example of groupthink than Hillaryland.

The curse of conformity is not peculiar to America's educated liberal class. In one way or another, the technocratic mindset has gripped political elites across the Western world. The late political scientist Peter Mair called it 'ruling the void'.[14] The more the established parties detached themselves from the societies in which they had once been anchored, the greater the indifference they generated. It is no accident that the heyday of stable Western party politics coincided with the post-war golden decades of the rising middle and working classes. Political parties were embedded in the churches, veterans' clubs and trade union halls of ordinary life. The Dutch called this 'pillarization'. But the success of centre-left parties in creating a ladder of class mobility, and opening up higher education to blue-collar families, through grand reforms such as the GI Bill, bred the conditions for the old left's demise. In America, the share of voters describing themselves as independent has been creeping up for years.[15] This is no measure of Socratic equidistance. For the most part, independent is a fancy word for apathetic. In Europe, the rate of party membership has been on the wane for a generation. At the peak in the early 1980s, almost a tenth of Europeans were paid-up members of a political party – and that did not include the millions more affiliated to centre-left parties via their trade union. That number has been cut in half.[16]

Starting with the Third Way in the 1990s, the left began to shed its old clothing. Voters ceased on any real scale to participate in the political process: instead they became consumers. Mair called this 'audience democracy'. In the British general election of 1964, the working classes outnumbered voters with professional qualifications by two to one. By 1997, when Tony Blair's Labour swept to power, they were level-pegging. Union membership had halved. Only one in twelve of those born before 1931 had a degree, compared with two out of three for those born since 1975.[17] Politics had to keep up. It would have been impossible for Tony Blair, or Bill Clinton for that matter, to win by indulging the old rhetoric of mass mobilisation. Pretty soon, the big parties began to look and sound alike. As Jan-Werner Müller put it, 'The third way turned elections into a mere choice between Coke and Pepsi.'[18] Elections went from win-lose to win-win in the mind of the elites. The party leaders went to the same schools and spoke in the same way. Paul Nuttall, leader of the UK Independence Party, put it like this: 'In the days of Clement Attlee [after the Second World War], the Labour MPs came from the mills, the mines and the factories. The Labour MPs today follow the same route as the Conservatives and the Liberal Democrats. They go to private school, they go to Oxbridge, they get a job in an MP's office and they become an MP. None of them would know what it's like in a working man's club.'[19]

For a while, the Third Way's appeal to aspirational voters paid dividends. After more than a decade in the wilderness, the Democrats and Labour regained power in the 1990s. In France, François Mitterrand had already performed this U-turn in the early 1980s. On the eve of the millennium, the Third Way leaders, among them Clinton and Blair, Germany's Gerhard Schröder, France's Lionel Jospin and Italy's Massimo D'Alema, met at a grand conference in Florence – a fitting Tuscan setting for such a celebratory gathering. Across the Western world, the new left had ushered in the dawn of the classless society. People talked of a post-ideological age. The Third Way had remade politics. Lip service was still paid to the blue-collar worker. But the new left's chosen politics was a form of anti-politics in which 'whatever works' had apparently replaced ideology. Beneath them was the void. 'I was never really in politics,' Blair told the BBC in 2000. 'I never grew up as a politician. I don't feel myself a politician even now.' All of which would have been fine if the blue-collar classes had disappeared. Many of their old jobs certainly did. But when the economic tide went out in 2008, it suddenly became clear how many people had been swimming naked. The left-behinds looked rather more numerous than the cosmopolitans had supposed. The difference was that they no longer had a party to speak for them. It was not just the economy that had left them stranded – the Clintons and the Blairs had moved along too. Having built their political careers on the aspirational vote, the Third Way leaders were unable to find the vocabulary to engage the losers. The new left had long since become fluent in McKinsey-speak – the lingua franca of Davos. When I sat down with Tony Blair in early 2016, he cheerfully admitted he had little idea why all the political turmoil was happening: 'I really mean it when I say that I'm not sure I fully understand politics right now, which is an odd thing to say when I've spent my life in it,' he said.[20]

This posed a far bigger headache for Mrs Clinton than for Tony Blair, since she was still running for office. One measure of her distance from the mood of the country in 2016 was captured in a leaked email listing her choice of election slogans. It would have made a second-rate advertiser wince. Of the eighty-four her team considered, 'It's your time', 'Time for a better bargain' and 'Our Families, Our Future' revealed an operation devoid of spark. My two favourites were 'Next begins with you' and 'It's about you. It's about time.' If you substitute 'me' for 'you', it will give you some idea how most Americans perceived Mrs Clinton. It marked the endpoint of an electoral strategy that no longer had anything new to say. The Third Way itself had been swallowed by the void. Like David Cameron's ill-fated Remain campaign in the UK, Clinton eventually settled on 'Stronger Together'. But she failed to articulate why. It seemed more like a game of demographic addition than a reason to govern. Meanwhile, much of her presumed base – the college-educated millennials – had defected to Bernie Sanders. One widely shared meme crystallised their view of Mrs Clinton. It showed a fake poster comparing the two candidates on the issue of whether they would dine at Olive Garden – a soulless restaurant chain that is popular in the suburbs. 'Only when I'm high,' says Sanders's caption. 'An authentic Italian restaurant for the whole family!' says Hillary. In the general election, the millennials stayed home in droves.

It was not that Hillary Clinton lacked policies. She had reams of them. But they were the *reductio ad absurdum* of an exhausted technocracy. Most of her policies would have complicated the US tax code even further with minutely precise tax breaks that only the upper classes – those who could afford to hire accountants – would be capable of exploiting. They had the least reason to bother. Here is a typical example. In response to Sanders's highly popular vow to pay for tuition at public universities, Mrs Clinton came up with a counter-plan, which would allow former students who had launched start-up businesses to defer their debt payments for up to three years. Her tax break would also be available to the company's first twenty employees. She also promised loan forgiveness of up to $17,500 for former students who either set up a new business in 'distressed communities' or 'social enterprises that provide measurable social impact'.[21] It is hard to imagine how Mrs Clinton's talented campaign staff could have come up with such a mess – and with such precision. Why $17,500 instead of $20,000? Why a ceiling of twenty employees, and not thirty? And who would measure the start-up's 'social impact'? Sanders had thrown down the gauntlet by promising free tuition for all. Mrs Clinton countered with moderate forgiveness for a certain type of good citizen who had time to file the claim while working day and night to start a new business – and in a tough neighbourhood! Her website listed bullet-point plans to solve forty-one measurable problems, each containing multiple sub-plans to solve multiple sub-problems.[22] There was even a plan to protect the interest of dogs, cats and horses. Desiccated manifestos might pass muster at the United Nations. But they do not inspire electorates. I could reprise the rest of Mrs Clinton's programme, but there would be little profit since even the policy wonks lost interest.

The more technocracy loses touch, the more it reaches for the remote control. The subtext of Mrs Clinton's campaign was that she was the harbinger of a new America in which whites were rapidly turning into a minority. Adapting to this new multicultural world would require an ongoing revision of our vocabulary – an expanding lexicon of political correctness. The campus movement to create 'safe spaces' protected from 'microaggressions' and issue literary 'trigger warnings' found its ultimate echo in the Clinton campaign. Yet the demography-as-destiny vision rests on highly dubious assumptions. The US census projects that America will become a minority-majority country by 2044, when whites drop to below half the population.[23] But that is only because Washington classifies Hispanics as non-whites, a revision that was made at the turn of the millennium. Until then, South Americans, Puerto Ricans and Cubans, for example, appeared separately on the census and could choose their race. But there is a wrinkle in the data, which belies the left's minority triumphalism. More than half of America's Hispanics consistently say they would prefer to call themselves white.[24] This is not just an abstract battle over classification. It means that many of those who are defined as Hispanic are no likelier to be natural Democrats than 'white' people (another contestable designation). It explains why many Hispanics reacted no differently during the election than most whites to Donald Trump's promised border wall. Mexican-Americans felt viscerally targeted by Trump. But there is little evidence to show that legal immigrants from other Spanish-speaking countries were any more outraged than any other voter. Why would the Democratic establishment bank more on their loyalty than it does on whites'? Resistance to such ethnic shoehorning might explain why a higher share of Hispanics voted for Donald Trump than had for Mitt Romney in 2012.[25]

If we took Hispanics at their word and treated more than half of them as white, America would remain a majority white country until at least the 2050s – and possibly indefinitely. Irish- and Italian-Americans were only accepted into the mainstream after the Second World War. It took just a few decades for them to shift from being reliably ethnic Democrats to forming the breakaway core of Reagan Democrats that realigned American politics. There is no reason to suppose 'Hispanics' will behave differently. The same might be said of the latest ethnic category, Middle East and North Africans (MENAs), which the Obama administration pushed through just before it left office.[26] At the stroke of a pen, the White House had conjured up ten million new non-whites. Again, the move betrayed a technocratic itch to channel people into corrals. Lebanese Christians and secular Turks may have less in common with Sudanese Muslims than with whites. Yet overnight they could benefit from the same affirmative action to enter university as other minorities. Hillary-land was inured to how badly this game of favourites came across to non-college-educated whites, who still form America's largest voting bloc, and will continue to do so for some time. A few weeks before the election Mrs Clinton described half of them as belonging in a 'basket of deplorables', whose racial prejudices would consign them to history's trashcan. In her otherwise gracious concession speech, Mrs Clinton reeled off all the Americans who had contributed to her coalition. This included 'people of all races and religions', 'immigrants', 'LGBT people', and 'people with disabilities'. Her list did not extend to the guy in the pick-up truck or the blue-collar labourer. They had been forgotten.

Failure to diagnose the reasons for Mrs Clinton's defeat will only make Trump's re-election more likely. In a searing piece for the *New York Times* after the election, Mark Lilla, a professor at Columbia University, called for an end to 'identity liberalism'. The American left had 'slipped into a kind of moral panic about racial, gender and sexual identity that has distorted liberalism's message,' he wrote.[27] Moreover, if the Democratic standard-bearer insisted on namechecking different groups at her rallies she had better mention everybody, otherwise those left out would feel resentful. Lilla also took issue with the liberal post-mortem on Mrs Clinton's defeat that laid the blame on a racially charged 'whitelash' against multicultural America – a verdict that was at odds with the revealed motivations of many Trump voters. 'This [post-mortem] is convenient because it sanctions a conviction of moral superiority,' wrote Lilla. 'It also encourages the fantasy that the Republican right is doomed to demographic extinction in the long run – which means liberals have only to wait for the country to fall into their laps.' As a professor of humanities in Manhattan, Lilla has impeccable liberal credentials. A colleague at Columbia nevertheless wrote a riposte to Lilla's piece that branded him a white supremacist.[28] Yet Lilla was on firm ground. Fascism is based on group rights. Liberal democracy is founded on individual rights.

The future of Western democracy looks bleak if American politics hardens into two racially hostile camps. Donald Trump consciously stokes racist sentiment, and has given a rocket boost to the 'alt-right' fringe of neo-Nazis and white nationalists. But to write off all those who voted for him as bigoted will only make his job easier. It is also inaccurate. Millions who backed Trump in 2016 had voted for Barack Obama in 2008. Did they suddenly become deplorable? A better explanation is that many kinds of Americans have long felt alienated from an establishment that has routinely sidelined their economic complaints. In 2008 America went for the outsider, an African-American with barely any experience in federal politics. Obama offered hope. In 2016 it went for another outsider with no background in any kind of politics. Trump channelled rage. To be clear: Trump poses a mortal threat to all America's most precious qualities. But by giving a higher priority to the politics of ethnic identity than people's common interests, the American left helped to create what it feared. The clash of economic interests is about relative trade-offs. Ethnic politics is a game of absolutes. In 1992, Bill Clinton won the overwhelming majority of non-college whites. By 2016, most of them had defected. Having branded their defection as racially motivated, liberals are signalling that they do not want them back. 'Liberals should bear in mind that the first identity movement in American politics was the Ku Klux Klan, which still exists,' wrote Lilla. 'Those who play the identity game should be prepared to lose it.'[29]

In one form or another, such brinkmanship now threatens almost every Western democracy. An eerily similar dialectic played out in Britain's 2016 Brexit referendum. Winston Churchill once joked that Britain and America were divided by a common language; today blue-collar whites on both sides of the Atlantic are speaking in the same idiom. They yearn for the security of a lost age. Just as America believed it had entered a post-racial era, Britain persuaded itself it had become a classless society. With a similar abandon to Mrs Clinton's 'deplorables' remark, David Cameron wrote off UKIP as a 'bunch of fruitcakes and loonies and closet racists'. This was an exaggeration – and also a counterproductive one. Britain's left-behinds are as alienated from twenty-first-century politics as their American counterparts, if not more so. London's elites are drawn from a far narrower pool than Washington's. What broadened UKIP's support beyond the fringes was its disdain for Britain's ruling classes. 'They are fed up to the back teeth with the cardboard cut-out careerists in Westminster,' said Nigel Farage, the former UKIP leader, of his party's voter base. 'The spot-the-difference politicians. Desperate to fight the middle ground, but can't even find it. Focus groupies. The triangulators. The dog whistlers. The politicians who daren't say what they really mean.'[30]

Britain's London-centric elites got into the habit of compartmentalising signs of a backlash. Cognitive dissonance is a powerful thing. Long before the 2016 referendum, there were plenty of signs that Britain's malaise went far deeper than the antics of fringe activists. In the 2001 general election, British voter turnout fell to an historic low of just 59 per cent. This ought to have sounded alarms. Much of the drop was due to rising apathy among working-class voters, who felt Labour put more energy into promoting multiculturalism than to addressing their concerns. It was easy to dismiss such complaints as racist. But immigration had soared from around three hundred thousand a year in the 1990s to more than half a million by the mid-2000s. At the turn of the century, just 11 per cent of British voters rated immigration as a top concern. That had jumped to almost a third a decade later.[31] Almost one in seven people living in Britain is now foreign-born, which is the same share as in America. In many council districts, the surge has overwhelmed the supply of public housing, school places and other scarce resources. When Gordon Brown encountered a voter during the 2010 election who complained about immigration, he described her as a 'bigoted woman'. His private remark was picked up by the microphone he was still wearing. A few weeks later, Labour was out of power. Cameron came into office vowing to cap net UK immigration at a hundred thousand a year – a promise he failed to keep. The year before the Brexit vote, the inflow topped three times that number. Successive US administrations have promised to enforce America's borders. They rarely do. Britain's record is little different. Sooner or later the established parties were likely to pay a price for writing off whole chunks of their electorates as bigoted.

Were they right nonetheless? Rumours of the death of racial prejudice have always been exaggerated. Yet racism is not the root cause of the rise of Western populism. UKIP undoubtedly attracts a lot of racist votes – and makes clever use of the dog whistle. Yet that does not mean all those who vote for it are racists. It is also careful to avoid going too far. When Farage and his colleagues debated the best name for their party in the 1990s, they rejected the word British since it overlapped with the overtly racist British National Party. Farage refers to the BNP as the 'Bloody Nasty Party'.[32] He pointed out that many of UKIP's potential voters were old enough to remember the Second World War and had a lifelong allergy to fascism. When Theresa May, then Home Secretary, set up a pilot scheme to round up illegal immigrants, he criticised her methods as 'nasty' and 'not the British way'. UKIP is officially opposed to 'unlimited mass immigration'. But for the most part, it has focused on stopping Britain from turning into 'a province of the United European superstate'. Only during the Brexit campaign did the party endorse overt xenophobia with its 'breaking point' poster showing hordes of Muslim immigrants streaming across the border. That did not deter a significant slice of the non-white electorate – particularly British Asians – from voting to leave Europe. Many of them, too, complained of having been squeezed out by the newcomers.

The populist right only began to do really well at the ballot box after they began to steal the left's clothes. In each case, including Donald Trump, populists broke with centre-right orthodoxy to argue in favour of a government safety net. This is what the old left used to promise and largely delivered (you might say over-delivered). It was the implicit bargain of modern Western democracy. In most countries, including the US, it took the form of social insurance. The link between the duties of citizenship and the right to draw benefits was a form of social contract. Even in relatively generous Sweden, future retirees must work for fifteen years before they are eligible to draw a pension.[33] It was an unfortunate coincidence that immigration started to surge just as the value of these benefits began to erode. That was a double whammy. The same governments that were cutting welfare payments were also allowing recent arrivals to join the system. It offended people's sense of fairness. 'You cannot cut entitlement spending and simultaneously widen access to them,' says Francis Fukuyama. 'Sooner or later, something has to give.'[34]

Academics call it welfare chauvinism.[35] Only after grasping its salience did the European right begin to take off. UKIP began life as an anti-tax small government party. Its share of the vote rarely crept above 1 per cent. The party became known as the home of disgruntled conservatives in the Home Counties. Now-adays it is an ardent defender of the National Health Service, with strongholds in working-class parts of northern England and the Midlands. UKIP's stark claim – or, more accurately, its outright lie – that Britain's exit from Europe would free up £350 million a week for NHS spending ('a new hospital every week') may have proved critical in tipping the referendum.

In continental Europe, the more generous the welfare system, the more bitter the reaction against immigrants. The Danish People's Party now takes more than a quarter of that country's once reliably social democratic working-class vote. In Holland Geert Wilders's Party for Freedom takes an even higher share. (Much as people prematurely celebrated the Austrian Freedom Party candidate's defeat in December as a blow against pop-ulism, Wilders's Party for Freedom's poor second-place showing in Holland in March came with a sting. The whole political spectrum had shifted towards Wilders's Islamophobic agenda.) France's National Front used to speak for the farmers and small businesses of *La France profonde*, which opposed high taxes. After Marine Le Pen took over the leadership, she converted it into a party of the working classes. In a sharp rupture from her Holocaust-denying father, Le Pen has set herself up as the defender of France's social contract against 'the Islamic occupa-tion' – a phrase that instantly brings to mind the Nazi occupa-tion. 'National solidarity is for the nationals,' she said.[36] Le Pen knows her market.

Donald Trump does too. He was the first Republican presidential nominee to promise to increase spending on Social Security, Medicaid and Medicare. It signalled he was a very different kind of conservative from anyone else in the field. Republicans ritually vow to reduce entitlements spending – as do many Democrats. Mrs Clinton simply offered to defend it. There is barely a wealthy American, liberal or conservative, who would dispute the need to cut entitlements spending, as Bush tried and failed to do. There are not many poor Americans, white or black, who would agree. George W. Bush once joked to an audience of wealthy diners, 'This is an impressive crowd – the haves and the have-mores. Some people call you the elites: I call you my base.' He was joking. Trump was deadly earnest when he said 'I love the poorly educated.' They *are* his base. In 2016, for the first time in US history, a majority of those who voted for a Republican candidate did not have college degrees.[37] Not all of them were white.

We like to believe that our democracies are sustained by a shared commitment to principle. In some respects that is true. But when growth vanishes, our societies reveal a different face. Without higher growth, the return of racial politics looks set to continue. Our ability to contain such tendencies may not be as sophisticated as we had thought. The battle is also generational. In both the US and the UK, younger, more racially diverse urban voters failed to turn out in anything like the numbers of older, whiter and more rural voters in 2016. These are foretastes of the deep splits that the decades of more broadly distributed growth made it possible to finesse. Following the Brexit vote, many British commentators openly speculated about whether the franchise should be curtailed for those who would not live to see the consequences of their decisions. The right to vote should be much like driving: when your aptitude declines, you lose your licence. It was only partly in jest.

More seriously, efforts to suppress the democratic franchise in many US states, particularly among African-Americans, have reached a pitch not seen since the civil rights era. Trump will make that drastically worse. In Enlightenment terms, our democracies are switching from John Locke's social contract to the bleaker Leviathan of Thomas Hobbes. We are on a menacing trajectory brought about by ignorance of our history, indifference towards society's losers and complacency about the strength of our democracy. It has helped turn society into a contest of ethnic grievances, in which 'awakened whites' – as the alt-right now call them – are by far the largest minority.

———

For decades, the French writer Didier Eribon disguised his humble origins. At some point during his upbringing on the grim housing estates that encircle Reims, he realised he was different from the rest of his family. His father was a factory worker who had left school at fourteen, like most of the working classes in post-war France. His mother was a cleaner. Their apartment was threadbare. Eribon would spend 'intolerable evenings' sitting around the black-and-white TV set watching football games. Periodically, his father would go to night school to try to improve his qualifications. But he was always too tired to do the homework. With a familiar sigh he would shove his papers to the bottom of the drawer, 'where he kept his broken dreams'. As life went on, he grew increasingly short-tempered and would shout at the slightest provocation. Once he attacked Eribon's mother with a kitchen knife. Eribon grew to hate his father.

Religion played very little role in his childhood. Like most of their neighbours, the Eribons were militantly anti-clerical. Occasionally his mother would treat the local church as a form of childcare. But his parents never attended mass. They saw Christianity as the opium of the masses. Their only real idea of community was political. The neighbourhood's sense of class consciousness was intense. Eribon's people divided the world into two camps: those who were for the workers, and those who were against. Everyone voted for the Communist Party candidate at every election. When the communist candidate would inevitably fail to make it to the second round of the presidential election – the party's peak was 21 per cent of the vote in 1977 – they would cast their lot with the socialist. 'We would explode with anger upon learning that the party of the right had won yet again,' says Eribon. On foreign policy, they would inevitably take the side of the Soviets against the Americans. They were not fans of Charles de Gaulle. This was Eribon's childhood. Politics was a glue that bound people together. 'To vote was to participate in an important moment of collective self-affirmation,' he writes in his extraordinary memoir, *Returning to Reims*.[38] 'It was a moment that affirmed your political significance.'

As he grew older, Eribon found an 'inner region' in himself that was quite different from what he was expected to be. In his mind he redefined himself as a gay teenager, rather than 'the son of a worker'. He also developed a passion for reading. Being a budding intellectual, his reading list was highly abstract. Volumes by Montaigne, Kant, Balzac and Aristotle sat by his bed. The steep demands of tomes such as *Dialectics of the Concrete* competed with Eribon's furtive trips to the streets behind the railway station, where gay men cruised the night. Occasionally he would get beaten up. His family could no longer relate to him. 'You talk like a book,' said his father. Technically, Eribon's politics remained the same as everyone else's. But the more he disdained the reality of his family life, the more he romanticised the working classes. He preferred Marxist theories on working-class 'spontaneous forms of knowledge' to the grim cultural poverty of those around him. On one occasion, when he brought a Trotskyite friend home, they tied his father up in knots arguing about politics. After the friend had left, Eribon's father railed against left-wing students who were always telling the working classes what to do. 'In ten years they will be coming back and giving us orders,' he said. Eribon had nothing but contempt for his father. He left to study in Paris aged nineteen and never saw him again. When Eribon's mother called thirty-five years later to say that his father was dying, he could not bring himself to visit him on his deathbed.

Eribon made his name in the 1980s with a widely acclaimed biography of Michel Foucault, the post-structuralist philosopher of post-war France, whose work on the diagnosis of the insane, and the boundaries societies drew around mental illness, shed light on the pathologies of what was considered normal. The intellectual Paris of the 1970s and the 1980s was the perfect venue to come out as gay. Eribon's left-wing friends were no longer much interested in the actual working classes, who, like Eribon's father, were homophobic and misogynistic. After François Mitterrand's government had made mincemeat of the Communist Party in the early 1980s and shifted French social-ism to the right, Eribon lost interest in the politics of his youth. Solidarity became a defunct term. Personal liberation was the new mantra. The term class even lost its salience. In this differ-ent world, Eribon's people were simply known as 'marginalised'. They would fade into history. Eribon, meanwhile, was ashamed of his background. 'I would often find myself lying ... about my class origins, or feeling embarrassed when admitting my back-ground in front of them,' he writes. 'I shut myself up in what might be called a "class closet".'

Once or twice he would be tugged back to his roots by a stray comment from one of his bourgeois friends. He found it hard to disguise his disdain for the way they posed at Parisian music recitals. Unlike Eribon, his friends had been taught how to listen. More precisely, they had learned how to appear to others while they were listening. Everyone pretended 'to be caught up in some kind of inspired reverie' when in fact, they were just as bored by the music as he was. His observation reminded me of J. D. Vance, the hillbilly author, whose girlfriend had to correct his eating habits when he was applying to Princeton. He had to be told to chew with his mouth closed. When he was offered a glass of sparkling water, 'I took one sip and literally spit it out.'[39] As Eribon explains, it is 'only when you have crossed from one side of the border to the other' – the line between two radically different worlds – that you realise how little social capital you possess. The advantages of being raised on the right side of the tracks are too implicit to be enumerated. It is the few who have escaped who grasp the full impotence of those they have left behind.

After his father died, Eribon finally returned to Reims. A Parisian friend asked him whether he would be present for the reading of the will. It brought home what a gulf he had crossed. 'What precisely would they [his family] be leaving to anyone?' he thought. Eribon found that little had changed. His mother still cleaned houses. One of his brothers still worked as a butcher. The other was still a policeman. Yet everything had changed. They no longer voted communist. Their new political church was Marine Le Pen's National Front. Eribon's mother complained about the 'swarms' of North African children on her staircase, and the strange noises and smells wafting into her flat. The word class may have been abolished, but its former occupants still existed. They had just transferred their collective loyalty. Instead of the workers versus the bourgeois, it was now the French against the foreigners. 'Right or left, there's no difference,' said Eribon's mother when he reproved her for her new voting habit. 'The same people always end up footing the bill.' The big difference was that they now had someone to look down upon. But shock gradually gave way to a grudging appreciation of the trials his family had endured. He also remembered what his father had predicted about the left-wing students coming back in ten years' time and telling him what to do. Those same people now ran the universities, the government, and managed the big factories. They had become defenders of a world perfectly suited to the people they had become. 'Nowadays,' asks Eribon, 'how is it possible to think my father was wrong?'

One weekend he took his mother to Paris. She wandered the streets staring at people as though she had landed on Mars. They say the past is another country – that was certainly true for Eribon. But for his mother it was the present that was foreign. Though she still avoided church, her new lodestar was Joan of Arc, the symbol of the National Front. Meanwhile, Eribon learned that his father had not been ashamed of him at all. One evening he had watched his son on national television talking about being gay. His eyes welled up as he realised someone in the family had finally made something of their life. He threatened to beat up anyone in the neighbourhood who said anything derogatory about his son's sexuality. It was only after his father died that Eribon finally let go of his hate and allowed the pain in. 'I regretted the fact that I hadn't tried to understand him – that I hadn't at some point tried to talk to him again. I regretted the fact that I had allowed the violence of the social world to triumph over me, as it had triumphed over him.' Eribon also finally came out from his class closet. He despises French neo-fascism. But he understands more about why people like his mother have strayed into its orbit: 'I am convinced that voting for the National Front must be interpreted, at least in part, as the final recourse of people of the working classes attempting to defend their collective identity, or to defend, in any case, a dignity that was being trampled on – even now by those who had once been their representatives and defenders.'[40]

Eribon's tale is about the elite left's divorce from the working classes. These elites were what Marx called the vanguard of the proletariat – the enlightened bourgeois who would lead their revolution. Nowadays Lenin would be teaching cultural studies at the Sorbonne. All traces of Marxist romanticism have been shed. So have the names. Working class has been supplanted by left behind. Once romanticised, they are now denigrated. But the elite leftists have only swapped one myth for another. There is nothing new about working-class populism. It can go in many directions depending on the situation. America's populist surge in the late nineteenth century produced both the Ku Klux Klan and the progressive income tax. The latter's champion, William Jennings Bryan, fought for the little guy who was being 'crucified on the cross of gold'. His followers hated 'the plutocrats, the aristocrats, and all the other rats'.[41] Bryan ended his career arguing against the theory of evolution as a prosecutor in the famous Scopes Monkey trial.

Eribon could also have been talking about the left-behinds in any Western democracy. Following Trump's victory, an Ancient Greek term suddenly re-entered English usage: *demophobia* – literally, fear of the mob. What it conveys is cold feet about democracy. Trump's ascendancy brought out the liberal technocrat in many people. 'I love America. It's Americans I hate,' wrote Tim Kreider, an essayist and cartoonist, a few weeks after Trump won.[42] '[They're] pathetically dumb and gullible, uncritical consumers of any disinformation that confirms their biases, easy dupes for any demagogue who promises to bring back the factories and keep the brown people down ... But I don't believe all Trump voters are ignorant, or bigoted; most of them are just evil – evil being defined not as anything so glamorous as beheading journalists or gunning down grade schoolers, but simply as not much caring about other people's suffering.' The Trump era's changing vocabulary also includes a word of more recent coinage: *oikophobia*, literally an aversion to home surroundings. In reality, it means fear of your own people – the opposite of xenophobia. The term was invented by Roger

Scruton, the conservative philosopher, to describe the global elitist who fears the provincial masses and looks down on their national loyalties. 'The oikophobe is, in his own eyes, a defender of enlightened universalism against local chauvinism,' Scruton said.[43] Only the word is new. In the US, poor whites have always been a class apart, second only to slaves and their descendants. In some ways the white degenerates of the Smoky Mountains and the swamplands were considered to be lower than slaves. Indeed, the term 'redneck' is thought to have been coined by slaves. As the sharecropper song went, 'I'd druther be a Nigger, an' plow ole Beck, Dan a white Hill Billy wid his long red neck.'[44] Variously, they have also been called lubbers, offscourings, crackers, hillbillies, clay-eaters, low-downers, degenerates, white niggers and trailer trash. The term white trash has been around for two centuries and is still very much in use.

America's Founding Fathers had such people in mind when they designed the US constitution. Their goal was to prevent the re-emergence of the tyranny of George III, although this time in the guise of the 'tyranny of the majority', as de Tocqueville put it. 'An elective despotism was not the government we fought for,' said Thomas Jefferson. Of America's three branches of government, just half of one – the House of Representatives – provided for direct election by the people. The presidency and the Senate only democratised gradually. The US Constitution would incubate a 'natural aristocracy of the talents', in Jefferson's view. Far from being democratic, this ingenious Heath Robinson contraption was designed to keep the mob out. In explaining the anomaly of having one branch of directly elected representatives, a signatory to the Philadelphia document explained that they had raised 'the federal pyramid to a considerable altitude, and for that reason wished to give it as broad a base as possible'.[45] It took several decades for suffrage to spread to the majority of white males, and only then by accident rather than design. The founders set the threshold at 'forty shilling freehold' but forgot to index it to inflation. As property values rose, so the electorate grew.

The first time America began to look like a mass democracy was with the election of Andrew Jackson in 1828, more than forty years after the republic's launch. If you cast around US history for a parallel to Trump, Jackson is the only clear answer you will find. America has had its share of demagoguery – Father Coughlin's anti-Semitic radio broadcasts in the 1930s and George Wallace's segregationalist poison in the 1960s among them. But Jackson was the only authentic populist to have made it to the White House. The similarities to Trump are striking. Apart from the fact Jackson was 'slightly over six feet tall … with a thick thatch of sandy red hair', he claimed to speak for the 'farmers, mechanics, and laborers' against the financial interests of the time.[46] Jackson's sympathy for the mob extended only to white males. He was a slaveholder and a very wealthy man.

Much like Trump, Jackson resented those above him and despised the people at the bottom. Those who considered themselves above Jackson got their comeuppance when he shut down the Second Bank of America – the US Federal Reserve of its day. Those beneath him, notably the Cherokee Indians, were uprooted from their homes in the largest transfer of a Native American people to date. It is hard to miss the parallel to Trump's plans to deport up to eleven million Mexican immigrants. Jackson treated any criticisms of his brutal policies as the crocodile tears of a hypocritical elite. Abolitionists were treated to particular scorn. The Jackson administration 'presumed the supremacy of whites over nonwhites, and interpreted any challenge to that supremacy as pretended philanthropy,' wrote Sean Wilentz, one of Jackson's biographers.[47] Jackson promised to clean 'the Giant Augean Stable at Washington' (Trump promises to 'drain the swamp'). Once in office he lost no time setting up America's spoils system in which government jobs were distributed to friends and supporters. In spite of his record, historians refer to Jackson's era as the age of democratic revolution – or simply the age of the common man.

Until just yesterday, it seems, Western elites only thought of democracy with instinctive pride. To question it would be as odd as denigrating clean air, or two-parent families. In the nineteenth century, the very word inspired fear, much as 'Bolshevism' frightened their twentieth-century descendants (my mother still occasionally refers to impolite people as 'bolshie'). Even the most self-improving Victorian liberals recoiled in horror at the notion the labouring classes would get to choose who governed Britain. It was only in the 1870s that the franchise was extended to a majority of white males. 'I can conceive of nothing more corrupting or worse for a set of poor ignorant people than that two combinations of well-taught and rich men should constantly offer to defer to their decision, and compete for the office of executing it,' wrote Walter Bagehot, the Victorian essayist, after whom an *Economist* column is named. '*Vox populi* will be *Vox diaboli* if it is worked in that manner.'[48] The most revealing aspect of Bagehot's fear was that he still could not conceive of the 'ignorant people' assuming office themselves.

It took a while for the privileged classes to acclimatise to the universal franchise. It took them still longer to think of it as a good thing. The first time the British government publicly championed the country as a democracy was in 1916, in the depths of the First World War, when it was grasping for a large enough cause to justify the deaths of hundreds of thousands of young men in the trenches. Britain's chief enemy, the Kaiser's Germany, was autocratic. One of Britain's main allies, Russia, pulled out of the war after its Tsar was overthrown (and then executed) in the Russian Revolution. After they had seized control, the Bolsheviks instantly became the new – and far more menacing – *bête noire* in the capitals of Europe. More democracy at home was suddenly an essential tool of survival. Woodrow Wilson, the US president, said America was entering Europe's great war in order to save democracy. That, too, was a novelty for Americans. It became second nature for the US, Britain and France – and, once the Cold War with the Soviets had begun half a generation later, the rest of western Europe – to hold up democracy as the crown jewel of Western civilisation. By historic standards, a hundred years is comparatively short. Another century might feel like a biblical leap of faith nowadays.

Even during the golden decades of democracy, the West was careful not to let direct democracy run away with itself. Most of post-Second World War Europe, led by Germany, designed constitutions with much the same motives in mind as America's Founding Fathers: fear of the undiluted voice of the people. Adolf Hitler, after all, attracted almost 40 per cent of the popular vote in the free election of 1932. The Austrians had voted overwhelmingly in a referendum for *Anschluss*. Much like Italy, Austria, Portugal and others, Germany's post-war constitution built in plenty of checks to limit the influence of the *Vox populi*. The presidency was a weak figurehead. The first line of Germany's 1949 Basic Law says 'Human dignity shall be inviolable. To respect and protect it shall be the duty of all state authority.' Government was to be not so much by the people, as for the people. Only in France, where Charles de Gaulle drew up a new presidential constitution in the 1950s, was the direct voice of the people viewed without dread. That was in spite of the fact that France's weak coalition governments had been plagued in the 1930s by the running street battle between homegrown fascists and communists. 'Better Hitler than Blum,' said the fascists of the coalition government led by Léon Blum, a socialist, who was also Jewish. France's semi-civil war paralysed its politics and fatally divided the country in the lead-up to the Second World War. Of the main Western democracies, only the US and Britain had managed to keep the extremists at bay. Even then, however, the mob was influential. The popularity of the America First movement led by the aviation celebrity Charles Lindbergh, who admired Nazi Germany – and whose rallying cry was lifted by Trump – contributed to America's near-fatal delay in entering into the Second World War. Britain's 1930s Conservative governments were hopelessly divided in their response to the rise of Nazi Germany. Some wished to avoid conflict at all costs after the carnage of the Great War. Others openly sympathised with Hitler's agenda. Even Winston Churchill, the great voice in the parliamentary wilderness, was supposed to have congratulated Mussolini for ensuring the trains ran on time.

Once the Iron Curtain descended on Europe in the late 1940s, the golden age of democracy got under way. So, too, did a process of historic amnesia. During the Cold War, the English-speaking democracies all but forgot their history of ambivalence towards the voice of the people. Since the end of the Cold War, fear of public opinion has crept back. Oikophobia is real. The feelings of the elites have become progressively more sceptical of democracy since the fall of the Berlin Wall. The period since then has coincided with the most dramatic expansion of the European Union. Not only did Europe's club almost double from fifteen to twenty-eight members (soon to be twenty-seven, after the completion of Brexit), but the powers concentrated in

Brussels grew dramatically. Whatever else you can say about the EU, it is not a democracy. 'European integration, it needs to be emphasized, was part and parcel of this comprehensive attempt to constrain the popular will,' says Harvard's Jan-Werner Müller.[49] 'It added supranational constraints to national ones.' The system of anonymous committees that set the rules for its member states – from the minutest product regulations to the limits of tax and spending – is virtually impervious to democratic control. They call it comitology. Only a tiny few understand Brussels's comitological system. The president of the European Commission is almost always a nonentity drawn from somewhere like Belgium or Luxembourg: easy for governments to control, never a household name. He presides over a Byzantium of layered bureaucracy that would have been familiar to Franz Kafka. It is ironic that Europe's powers have metastasised so far since the Soviet threat receded. 'Why, just as democracy seemed to triumph, did there emerge a concern to limit its scope?' asked Peter Mair, author of *Ruling the Void*.

A year after the fall of the Berlin Wall, I took a traineeship in Brussels at the European Commission – a *stagiare*, as it is called. Although I was a supporter of the European project, those six months inoculated me for life against working in a bureaucracy. It was a stifling experience. Journalism promised wind in my hair on an open road. A university friend urged me to look up his brother, a British journalist who had made his reputation lampooning the ways of Brussels. His name was Boris Johnson. His trade was slanted reporting. It was 'better to be pissing in from the outside than pissing out from the inside', Boris joked, paraphrasing Lyndon B. Johnson's famous quip. Though I disagreed with Boris's politics and his journalistic methods – he specialised in mischievous caricature – it was easy to see why he had gained such a following in the UK. A quarter of a century later, Boris played a starring role in Britain's vote to exit from Europe. The mandarins of Brussels, like Hillaryland, are blind to how people perceive them. Brexit has only reinforced their worldview. The verdict in Brussels is that Britain's exit is an opportunity. It will allow European integration to pick up more speed. It is an open question whether Brussels's response will trigger more Brexits in the years ahead. The same obliviousness applies to Washington, where I have lived for the past decade. Ninety-one per cent of Washington voted for Hillary Clinton in 2016. Trump's victory has only bolstered the view that people outside the capital's beltway are ignorant and malevolent.

The term illiberal democracy was devised by Fareed Zakaria more than a decade ago. The public's idea of democracy is that it is a simple process in which people elect their representatives to carry out their instructions. Scholars call this the 'folk theory of democracy'.[50] It is an updated view of the faith medieval peasants placed in their monarch. If the king was ignoring them it must be because he had bad advisers. Simply update the divine right of kings with the divine right of the people: 'The people are never corrupted, but sometimes deceived.' More and more people feel they are being tricked. Politicians promise one thing and do another. Resentment has grown steadily over the last two decades, in the US and elsewhere. The public's trust in political institutions has fallen to an all-time low. The sophisticated view of democracy is that it can only work if it is checked by a system of individual rights, independence of the judiciary, the separation of powers and other balances. There is no such thing as the popular will, just a series of messy deals between competing interests. It is hard to watch any legislature making laws without thinking the whole business is corrupt. As Bismarck put it, 'Laws, like sausages, cease to inspire respect in proportion as we know how they are made.' I have watched my fair share of sausage-making in the European Commission and on Capitol Hill. It's enough to put you off eating pork for good. Yet it is the only alternative to rule by dictatorial fiat.

The story of liberal democracy is thus a continual tension between the neat democratic folk theory and the more complex liberal idea. Nowadays they have turned into opposing forces. Here, then, is the crux of the West's crisis: our societies are split between the will of the people and the rule of the experts – the tyranny of the majority versus the club of self-serving insiders; Britain versus Brussels; West Virginia versus Washington. It follows that the election of Trump, and Britain's exit from Europe, is a reassertion of the popular will. In the words of one Dutch scholar, Western populism is an 'illiberal democratic response to undemocratic liberalism'.[51] The British and American people supposedly reclaimed their sovereignty in 2016. I call it the Reaction. It is pretty clear which direction the Western elites are bending. Davos is no fan club for more democracy. Having hived off many areas that were once under democratic control (such as monetary policy and trade and investment), post-2016 Western elites now fear they have not gone far enough.

But elite disenchantment with democracy has been rising for many years. According to the World Values Survey, which offers the most detailed take on the state of global public opinion, support for democracy has plummeted across the Western world since the fall of the Berlin Wall.[52] This is particularly true of the younger generations. For a long time, academics assumed that rising signs of disaffection with democracy were simply a reflection of dislike of the government of the moment. Government legitimacy may have been on the wane, but regime legitimacy was still robust. There were no alternatives. Democracy, after all, was the only game in town. That reading was far too complacent. When asked on a scale of one to ten how essential it was for them to live in a democracy, almost three-quarters of Americans born before the Second World War give it a ten. Democracy is something of a sacred value to the generation who fought against fascism – or suffered under it – and lived through the Cold War. Near-similar levels of support apply to their European counterparts, and to baby-boomers. For millennials, the opposite holds. Fewer than one in three American and European millennials answer ten. Yet when people under thirty were asked the same question in the mid-1990s, they gave a very high priority to living in a democracy. More than anyone, it is the people who have grown up since then who have lost faith in democracy.

Many millennials *do* think there are viable alternatives, including military government. One in six people of all ages in America and Europe now believe it would be a good or a very good thing for the 'army to rule'. That has risen from one in sixteen in the mid-1990s – a near trebling. Similar responses hold when people are asked if they would support a 'strong leader who doesn't have to bother with parliament and elections'. In Europe, the sharpest jumps in support for authoritarianism came in the most mature democracies, notably Britain and Sweden. But the most troubling finding is how sharply the rich have lost faith in democracy across the West as a whole. In the 1990s, the wealthy backed democracy more strongly than any other income group in America and Europe. That has turned upside down. The poor are now democracy's strongest fans, the rich its biggest sceptics. In 1995, just 5 per cent of wealthy Americans believed army rule would be a good thing. By 2014 that had more than tripled. An even higher share of upper-income millennials support autocracy. People tend to form political beliefs in their early years and then stick with them for life. If today's rich young are tomorrow's thought leaders, democracy has a shaky future. This survey's data only goes up to 2014. If it had been taken after Trump and Brexit, the gulf between how rich and poor see democracy would be even wider.

The more unequal societies become, the more likely we are to hear from the demophobes. This would strike a chord with my great-grandparents' generation. It would also sound familiar to America's Founding Fathers. 'The newfound aversion to democratic institutions among rich citizens in the West may be no more than a return to the historical norm,' write Yascha Mounk and Roberto Stefan Foa.[53] To put it more bluntly: when inequality is high, the rich fear the mob. In early 2016 I had an eye-popping conversation with a very big name from New York. He argued that there should be a general knowledge test for voters to screen out all the 'low-information voters'. He estimated the franchise test would cut the electorate in half. This would be a good thing. 'If we had a simple knowledge test we wouldn't have to worry about Trump becoming president,' he said. The test would work much like the floor that Madison, Jefferson and others set in the late eighteenth century – only it would be based on knowledge rather than property. Very twenty-first-century.

As we cross the frontier to swarm drones and robot soldiers, the rich will have less need of large-scale civilian armies – a key reason they expanded the franchise in the nineteenth and twentieth centuries. Science fiction likes to depict a dystopia in which the robots have taken over. A less fantastical idea is that the robots will indeed take over. But it will be at the behest of a narrow elite of human masters.[54]

One of Donald Trump's favourite activities is to watch pro-wrestling contests. Over the decades he has appeared multiple times as a star in his own right at World Wrestling Entertainment fights. Though America's future president never fought, he often entered the ring to participate in its hammed-up scripts. His most recent appearance was in 2015, shortly before he launched his presidential candidacy, when he helped pin down a mock-struggling Vince McMahon, the chief executive of WWE. To whooping crowds, he then shaved McMahon's head with an electric razor. Having finished the job, he turned to the baying crowd and pumped his fist in the air: 'Yeah!' said Trump. He clearly loved every minute of it. It is safe to say that Trump is the first US president to have entered a WWE ring. Is it too much to hope he will be the last? Vince and Linda McMahon, the couple who became very wealthy through WWE, which they launched in 1980, have given $5 million to the Trump Foundation. They also contributed to Trump's presidential campaign. In January 2017, Trump nominated Linda McMahon as the head of the Small Business Administration. In addition to making her fortune in WWE, McMahon is a strong advocate of education reform. Her assets added to a Trump cabinet with an estimated collective worth of more than $13 billion.[55]

The WWE is to US popular culture what bear-baiting was to medieval Europe. The difference is that it is all a big pretence. The audience knows the drama is staged. But it happily allows itself to get sucked in. They are just as emotionally invested as diehard soap-opera fans. WWE gives you villains, heroes, anti-heroes and victims. Tracking the WWE's changing scripts is a barometer of middle America's darker preoccupations. During the 1980s, the fights were about good versus evil. The latter would invariably have Russian, or perhaps Iranian, accents. They would eventually lose. Often the baddie would break down and confess how evil he was. After the Cold War, the stories began to change. Good and evil were replaced with dramas based on nasty personal disputes. The foreign enemy was supplanted by those around us. Victims would take revenge on their abusers. Vince McMahon increasingly starred as a greedy boss in the off-ring segments, which would be broadcast from a locker room or executive office via a large screen to the ringside audience. He played the grasping chief executive who was always trying to cheat or exploit the wrestlers he employed.

The most striking change is the disappearance of heroes. Everyone has some tawdry angle. No one is trustworthy. 'City after city, night after night, packed arena after packed arena, the wrestlers play out a new, broken social narrative,' writes Chris Hedges in *Empire of Illusion*.[56] 'It is about personal pain, vendettas, hedonism, and fantasies of revenge, while inflicting pain on others. It is the cult of victimhood.' Hedges was writing in 2009. Since then, WWE's popularity has been overtaken by the Ultimate Fighting Championship, which attracts tens of millions of viewers and earns its biggest stars tens of millions of dollars. Unlike wrestling, the UFC is not scripted. The contestants fight it out in a large octagonal steel cage. They really do aim to hurt each other. UFC fighters use a mixture of boxing and martial arts, including Thai kickboxing. Real blood flies around the ring. Teeth are occasionally knocked out. The victor typically issues repeated punches to the head of the floored loser before the referee intervenes. The official list of fouls includes biting, eye-gouging and head-butting. It makes scripted pro wrestling seem almost quaint. Trump helped promote some UFC events in their early years and was also involved in a short-lived rival franchise. One imagines he would enjoy the spectacle. The UFC is to popular culture what Trump is to politics – a brutal and unforgiving breed of show business. In place of solidarity, it offers the catharsis of revenge.

Against the plebeian fears of most of America's Founding Fathers ran a more idealistic faith in the native wisdom of the people. This sprang from Rousseau and Kant, who believed in humanity's innate moral compass – the popular common sense that was celebrated by Thomas Paine. The twentieth century destroyed whatever illusions Europeans harboured about Rousseau's general will. Yet in America, which has never suffered from the terror of organised demagoguery, there are fewer trip-wires. De Tocqueville's most acute insights on America were about its 'democracy of manners'. The aristocratic Frenchman, whose travels coincided with Andrew Jackson's presidency, did not fear a totalitarian future but a more insidious one that would emerge from the breast of our democratic temper. 'The nations of our time cannot prevent the conditions of men from becoming equal,' de Tocqueville wrote, 'but it depends upon themselves whether the principle of equality is to lead them to servitude or freedom, to knowledge or barbarism, to prosperity or wretchedness.'[57]

Even during the shock of Trump's victory, people reassured me that he would crumble under the weight of his own fantasies. The illusions that sweep populists to power can rarely survive much contact with the reality of governing. Trump would be no exception. But the wish is often father to our thoughts. We underestimate humanity's endless appetite for distraction. In 1996, Nicholas Negroponte, one of the earliest evangelists for the internet, proclaimed its liberating potential. He said, 'the role of the nation-state will change dramatically and there will be no more room for nationalism [on the internet] than there is for smallpox'.[58] Negroponte could no more imagine Trump as the product of the internet than identity theft. Yet here we are. To be sure, we can download the libraries of the world. We can also stream UFC. The same utopian leaps of faith recur with each new technological breakthrough. In the 1850s, the telegraph was proclaimed as the great unifier of humanity. 'It is impossible that old prejudices and hostilities should any longer exist,' said an editorial in the *New Englander*.[59] Henry David Thoreau had a more realistic grasp of its potential: 'We are in great haste to construct a magnetic telegraph from Maine to Texas,' he wrote, 'but Maine and Texas, it may be, have nothing important to communicate.'[60] Almost carbon-copy utopian claims were made of television, commercial air travel and the car. Now that we had the means to explore other cultures, barriers to understanding would come tumbling down. Guglielmo Marconi, one of the early radio tycoons, said 'the coming of the wireless era will make war impossible, because it will make war ridiculous'.[61] In addition to Churchill and Roosevelt, Hitler and Stalin became masters of that medium. Now we must believe that Trump's conspiracy theories will wither under the scrutiny of a million online citizen fact-checkers.

But what if his supporters do not care? What if middle America has become so cynical about the truth that it will take its script from a political version of pro wrestling? Orwell envisioned a future in which an all-seeing dictatorship would stamp out free thinking and outlaw human intimacy. But the internet has given us something far closer to Aldous Huxley's *Brave New World* than *Nineteen Eighty-Four*. Sales of both books shot up the charts after Trump was elected (along with Hannah Arendt's *The Origins of Totalitarianism*). Orwell's fear was that Big Brother would always be watching you. Huxley's dread was that we would be too busy watching *Big Brother* on TV to care. There is no need to ban books if people are not reading them. If the people are entertained, they will also be docile. In the movie *Gladiator*, Senator Gracchus, played by Derek Jacobi, understands that patrician defenders of the Roman Republic, such as him, are weak competitors to Emperor Commodus's bread and circuses. 'The beating heart of Rome is not the marble of the Senate, it's the sand of the Colosseum,' he says. 'He'll bring them death – and they will love him for it.' Vladimir Putin is a better student of Huxley than Orwell. When he was a KGB agent based in Dresden in the 1980s, most of its population could pick up television from the West on their transmitters. These were the most politically quiescent parts of East Germany. Far from being glued to the West German news, they were hooked on *Dallas*, *Baywatch* and *Dynasty*. As Evgeny Morozov pointed out in *The Net Delusion*, there was one part of the east that could not receive West German TV. It was known as the Valley of the Clueless. Yet it was also the most politicised part of the country. People from here applied in far higher numbers for exit visas than their supposedly better-informed neighbours. Sometimes the illusion of freedom is all people need.

Putin, who is the only world leader Trump admires, has applied these lessons well in today's Russia. The media is relatively free. Unlike in China, where the Great Firewall blocks a lot of Western media, most Russians have access to most global news sources. Sometimes a journalist is bumped off. Others are intimidated. More often, they are co-opted by the Russian state. Putin may have grasped something that has eluded the net evangelists, who had a strong influence in Mrs Clinton's State Department. The utopians believe the Revolution will be Twittered.[62] Putinists believe they are far too happy digesting Western entertainment to bother. Far from reading dissident blogs, Russians are just as enamoured of kittens and listicles. Such sites are where the bulk of our traffic goes. There is no reason to think Westerners are inherently savvier than their Russian counterparts. '[The] new Kremlin won't make the same mistake the old Soviet Union did: it will never let TV become dull,' writes Peter Pomerantsev. 'Most [Russians] are happy with the trade-off: complete freedom for complete silence.'[63]

Short of martial law, the US media is highly unlikely to be silenced, or co-opted, by Trump. When Steve Bannon, Trump's senior White House adviser, who helped pioneer much of the fake news that helped Trump to win, told Washington's journalists to shut up, he was met with derision.[64] Yet he was echoing a popular view in the heartland about an industry that has suffered an even steeper fall in its credibility than the political classes. If the US media is now the opposition party, as Bannon put it, where will the people stand? Again, Russia offers troubling signposts. When Putin won his thumping presidential victory in 2012 with more than two-thirds of the vote, he had little need of ballot-stuffing. Much like London's vote against Brexit, or Washington's endorsement of Hillary Clinton, more than half of Moscow voted against Putin. The gulf between America's metropolitan elites and those outside of the cities is no less wide than that between Moscow and its vast hinterlands. Putin's mastery of reality TV, an industry that is scripted by the Kremlin, and by its business acolytes, outweighs whatever cynicism he generates in the cities. Whether it is taking his shirt off to go hunting, or zooming onto the stage on a Harley and in Ray-Bans at the opening of the Winter Olympics, Putin's shape-shifting appearances are calibrated for the Russian left-behinds. They call the Kremlin's PR managers political technologists. Before taking office, Mr Trump was already America's celebrity apprentice-in-chief. Political technology is as much his friend as his enemy. The counter-revolution can also be tweeted.

If we cannot bank on the truth to hold Trump to account, can we rely on the system? The short answer is that we will find out. The longer one is that America's separation of powers, like any constitutional democracy, is upheld by the people who lead it. Top of the pyramid is the president himself. If the president has integrity, most of the rest falls into place. In Trump's Washington we must look for salvation further down the pecking order. Richard Nixon, who believed whatever the president did was by definition legal, was not felled by an abstract system. When he ordered the Brookings Institution to be burgled, Nixon's staff did not report him to the police. When he told the Pentagon to put US nuclear forces on high alert, he was not rebuffed. In both cases, Nixon's staff left his orders in abeyance overnight in the hope that he would be sober by the morning. In other cases, however, Nixon's senior staff willingly carried out law-breaking at his bequest, including the burglary of the Democratic offices in the Watergate complex. Had it not been for Mark Felt, the number-two official at the Federal Bureau of Investigation, Nixon's presidency might well have survived. Felt leaked details of

Nixon's law-breaking to Bob Woodward and Carl Bernstein at the *Washington Post*, which, in turn, had the courage to publish the story in spite of escalating White House threats.

In other cases, such as the unsung story of Randolph Thrower, senior officials refused to carry out Nixon's orders. As head of the Internal Revenue Service, Thrower was asked by Nixon's aides to audit politicians and journalists who were on Nixon's enemies list. Thrower, who died in 2014 aged one hundred, baulked at the order.[65] He then requested a meeting with Nixon to discuss his misgivings. Nixon refused to meet him. Five days later Thrower was fired. Nixon made clear to his aides what kind of replacement he wanted. 'I want to be sure he is a ruthless son of a bitch,' he was recorded as saying, 'that he will do what he's told, that every income tax return I want to see I see, that he will go after our enemies and not go after our friends.'[66] They came up with Johnnie M. Walters, who was considered more pliable than Thrower. In 1972 Walters was handed a list of two hundred of Nixon's enemies to investigate. He went to George Shultz, then US Treasury Secretary, to ask what to do. Shultz told him to lock the names in a safe. Walters instead handed the list to a staff member in Congress. 'Why the hell did we promote him?' said Nixon on being told of Walters's refusal to follow orders. Later Walters publicly testified to Congress on what he had been asked to do. Like Thrower, Walters lived to a ripe old age. He died a few years ago at the age of ninety-four. Perhaps clear conscience is a key to longevity.[67]

There is no way of knowing how many Felts, Throwers and Walterses are lurking in Trump's Washington. But their stories remind us that it is character, rather than laws, which upholds a system. If America's rule of law is to survive whatever Donald Trump throws at it, individuals will have to take risks with their careers. Will it be James Comey, head of the FBI, whose last-minute intervention in the campaign helped tip it Trump's way? Comey was panicked by Trump into issuing his statement about the re-opening of the FBI investigation into Mrs Clinton's emails. His lapse was a result of Trump having already singled him out as part of a 'rigged system'. In a country so viscerally divided, neutrality is treated as collusion. When one side in a democracy throws around pre-emptive charges of treason – and there is none higher than allegations of rigging a presidential election – the ground on which the law stands shrinks. It is harder to uphold blind justice when there is a storm howling around you. Comey lost his shirt in the gale. That was during an election that Trump was expected to lose. How much greater will the pressure be on Comey, or the IRS Commissioner – or the heads of the US intelligence agencies, for that matter – now that Trump is their commander-in-chief? As Machiavelli said, it is better for a prince to be feared than loved.

Then there is Congress, America's first branch of government. Given Capitol Hill's poor record of oversight, it would have to step up its game immeasurably. Washington's 'deep state' – the panoply of intelligence and national security

agencies that always seem to grow no matter which administration is in office – has run rings around Congress for years.[68]
Although Congress is supposed to oversee their activities, they
rely entirely on the agencies themselves to keep them informed.
In practice, the intelligence agencies brief only eight lawmakers
and usually only after the fact. They are not allowed to bring
aides or notes. 'We are like mushrooms,' says Norman Mineta, a
former US lawmaker. 'They keep us in the dark and feed us a lot
of manure.' Yet, as it showed in the Watergate hearings, and the
reforms that followed Nixon's resignation, Congress is capable
of checking a wayward executive branch. Again, though, it is
individuals, rather than the institution, that make the difference. If I were a budding Mark Felt, I would leak my material
to John McCain, the ornery senator from Arizona, or his fellow
Arizonian Jeff Flake, or Lindsey Graham, the Republican from
South Carolina. There are few who revile Trump more than the
Republican hawks.

Finally, there is the judiciary, America's third branch of government. There is nothing to stop a US president from ignoring
the courts. Pretending otherwise has been a civic duty of almost
every US president, barring Nixon. Andrew Jackson was also
an exception. When John Marshall, the great US Chief Justice,
issued a stay on Jackson's plans to uproot the Cherokee Indians,
Jackson said, 'Now let him enforce it.' The courts never did. It
is the president, not the judiciary, who controls the firepower.
Presidential constraint is the most essential ingredient of the

proper functioning of the American system. Here, too, character is the ultimate key. Readers who have made it this far need no disquisition on the content of Mr Trump's character. Yet I cannot resist re-telling one of Trump's favourite anecdotes. It is about the woman and the snake. Trump repeated it many times on the campaign trail. A 'tender-hearted' woman finds a wounded snake on the road. She takes it in and nurses it back to health. Having revived, the snake then turns and bites her. The dying woman asks why. 'Oh, shut up, silly woman,' says the reptile. 'You knew damn well I was a snake before you took me in.'[69]

Trump retold this fable as a warning against America taking in refugees from Syria. But it fits better as a morality tale on Trump's election. During the campaign, one journalist summarised the gap between the heartland view of Trump, and that of the liberal elites as follows: 'the press take him literally, but not seriously; his supporters take him seriously, but not literally'.[70] It turns out that both were wrong. Trump should have been taken seriously and literally. As became clear in his inaugural address, Trump's campaign promises were made in deadly earnest. Within days of taking office, he issued an executive order banning refugees from Syria. It turns out Trump's promise to ban Muslims from entering the US was also real. So too, I believe, was his vow to deport millions of Mexican immigrants. Then there were his promises to launch a trade war with China, unscramble the Western Nato alliance, forge a partnership with

Putin, and so on. Who will be Trump's Deep Throat? Where will we find his Mark Felt? The future of the world's largest democracy – and of global democracy in general – lies in the hands of people whose names we probably do not know.

———————

In the mid-1990s, I spent two years as the *Financial Times*'s correspondent in Manila. Although the Philippines had suffered for much of the previous generation under the thumb of Ferdinand Marcos, it was South-East Asia's freest state, having restored its democracy in the People Power Revolution of 1986. One of the country's downsides was crime. In addition to democracy, the Philippines inherited a promiscuous gun culture from the United States, which ruled the country for half a century. One weekend I flew down to the city of Davao, where I had heard about its mayor's unprecedented crime-control methods. The mayor, flanked by a posse of goons in B-movie shades and cowboy boots, took me to a shooting range. He handed me a revolver and told me to hit a target. I had no idea how much the pistol would kick and missed the target repeatedly, provoking gales of laughter from his entourage. Later, when I asked the mayor how he had got crime down so low, he said that local criminals had a taste for flying. One solution was to take them up in a helicopter and simply help them on their way. 'They never fly again,' he chuckled. I still get shivers when I think of how much laughter that provoked. The mayor's name was Rodrigo Duterte. He is now president of the Philippines.

If you want a case study in illiberal democracy, Duterte's Philippines would be a good place to start. More than seven thousand Filipino 'drug addicts' have lost their lives in the nine months since he was elected. Some human rights groups estimate the death toll is considerably higher. Often the corpses are found in the gutter, a bullet in their head, after an encounter with the police. Some 'commit suicide' in jail. In reality, many are probably not drug addicts, or drug dealers, at all. Duterte's blanket call on society, and even family members, to 'go ahead and kill them yourselves' has served as a cover for all sorts of score-settling. Yet Duterte's approval ratings have stayed at stratospheric levels by any Western standards. Around the world, only Vladimir Putin and Recep Tayyip Erdoğan, Turkey's democratically elected strongman, enjoy ratings of 80 per cent or more. Like Putin, and Trump, Duterte has the knack of finding the demotic pulse. Now, like Erdoğan, he is talking of amending the Philippine constitution to make it more plebiscitary. Activist judges, and liberal activists, are powerless in the face of a popular demagogue. After all, Duterte is acting in the name of the people.

Intellectuals have been debating the limits to the popular will for almost three thousand years. We have yet to improve on many of the Ancient Greek arguments. Plato believed that democracy was the rule of the mob – literally *demos* (mob) and *kratos* (rule). In his view, the mob could not distinguish between knowledge and opinion. Aristotle's answer was to combine the rule of the knowledgeable with the consent of the many. He also believed in constant rotation. Citizens should simply draw lots to decide who would occupy public roles. '[Rights] were only earned by being an active citizen, certainly not a sit-back-and-beg modern consumer democracy,' wrote the late Bernard Crick, one of Britain's deepest thinkers on democracy.[71] The Ancient Greeks and America's Founding Fathers would find nothing to like in Duterte's Philippines and Trump's America. Yet the ancients were setting the bar very high. Expecting an active citizenry is hardly practical in a democracy of 100 million people, such as the Philippines – still less in a country of 324 million. In ancient Athens, you could stare into the whites of your ruler's eyes. Fewer than one in a hundred Americans are ever likely to glimpse Trump in the flesh. Yet he claims to know who they are. 'The silent majority is back, and it is not silent,' said Trump. 'It is aggressive.'

Is illiberal democracy a contradiction in terms? Maybe not in its opening stages. But as time goes on, the true populist loses patience with the rules of the democratic game. Of the West's leaders, Hungary's Viktor Orbán has taken matters the furthest. It no longer makes sense to talk of Hungary as a bona fide democracy. Having rewritten the country's constitution to suit his party, and rushed it through on a low-turnout referendum,

Hungary's opposition faces an impossibly tilted playing field. The chances that Orbán's opponents could win an election under these conditions are slim to vanishing. Orbán now boasts that Hungary is an 'illiberal democracy'.

In his masterful survey of populism, Jan-Werner Müller takes up cudgels against those who argue populism is democratic. A true populist is not just opposed to the elites, he is also an enemy of pluralism. Without a plural society democracy loses its foundation. The populist never says 'We are the 99 per cent,' as Occupy Wall Street did during its Zuccotti Park protests. The populist claims to speak exclusively for the 100 per cent. Only they can know the identity of the true people. The Finnish populists began life as the True Finns. Today they are simply the Finns. The change of name is a measure of their success. 'The only important thing is the unification of the people – because the other people don't mean anything,' said Trump. It follows that Trump, like Orbán, is an authentic populist. He, and only he, can identify the true Americans.

What happens in Trump's America will supply much of the answer to Fukuyama's question of whether the world's democratic recession turns into a depression. But what happens in Europe matters too. Having arrogated most of the big decisions to itself, Brussels has left little more than identity politics to its member states. For the first time in its post-Nazi history, Germany will almost certainly see a far-right party clear the 5 per cent threshold to gain seats at its next general election.

The Alternative für Deutschland party is running at about 15 per cent in the polls. If Europe is to survive, its German centre must hold. Even if it does, things may still fall apart on the periphery. Will Turkey leave Nato? Can Britain stay in one piece? Can Belgium and Spain remain whole? Will Europe stem the swelling tide of migrants from Africa and the Middle East? Can the West regain its role as beacon to the world? Democracy activists in China are no longer so certain what they should believe. They are still in shock at Trump's victory. By contrast, Russia's dissidents long since abandoned the illusion that the West was helping their cause. In contrast to what they expected in the 1990s during Russia's transition to democracy, the traffic is now two-way. If political influence were measured in dollars, Russia earned a thumping surplus in 2016. Nowadays London is the place where Russia's oligarchs park their money. The terms of trade have shifted. 'If once upon a time they [Russian dissidents] used the phrase "the West" in general, and the word "London" in particular, to represent the beacon of what they aimed towards,' says Pomerantsev, 'now the words "London" and "the West" can be said with a light disgust, as the place that shelters and rewards and strengthens the very forces that oppress them.'

Since the start of this century, the West has forfeited much of its prestige. Our political model is no longer the envy of the world. As Western democracy has come into question, so too has its global power. America's loss has been relative: its share of world GDP has declined. It has also devalued its global credibility by prosecuting reckless wars in the false name of democracy. Europe's geopolitical loss has been absolute. It is barely any longer capable of projecting power beyond its own borders. Indeed, the very openness of Europe's borders presents a growing threat in itself. The world's centre of gravity, meanwhile, is shifting inexorably towards the east.

PART THREE

FALLOUT

All under heaven is great chaos. The situation is excellent.

CHOU ENLAI

Though anyone with eyes should have seen it coming, the US–China war of 2020 still caught us unawares.* Within days of defeating Hillary Clinton, President-Elect Trump threw down the gauntlet to China. Not only did he accept a congratulatory call from Taiwan's president, in itself a provocative departure, he also threatened US recognition of Taiwanese independence as a bargaining chip in his coming trade showdown. To be sure, Washington's foreign policy experts instantly grasped how reckless this was. Since 1979, America – and most of the rest of the world – has accepted the 'One China' policy that entailed exclusive recognition of China. But the rest of us

_____

* The US–China war scenario I sketch out is *not* a prediction. It is meant as a plausible extrapolation of the direction in which Trump is taking US foreign policy.

were slow to pick up on its implications. This was Trump messing with his Twitter account, we reassured ourselves. The system will guide him to a safer place once he takes office. Even after Trump delivered the most incendiary inaugural address in US history we still reached for our comfort blankets. Though Trump escalated his 'America first' rhetoric, vowed America would 'start winning again', and promised to 'protect our borders from the ravages of other countries', we knew his wasn't the true voice of America. Americans prefer speeches that appeal to the 'better angels of our nature', as Abraham Lincoln did in 1861, or 'pay any price, bear any burden, meet any hardship, support any friend', as John F. Kennedy promised a century later. If nothing else, public opinion would bring Trump around. Little did we notice that 51 per cent of Americans thought Trump's speech was 'optimistic', and 49 per cent who saw it rated it as 'good', or 'excellent'.[1] Who was cherry-picking the news? Was it Trump? Or us?

Looking back on it, of course, the war now seems to have been inevitable. Though Trump reluctantly endorsed a 'One China' stance a few weeks after taking office, and welcomed Xi Jinping to his 'Winter White House' at Mar-a-Lago two months after that, the genie was already out of the bottle. Indeed, with a US destroyer at the bottom of the South China Sea and large-scale US strikes on China's naval bases, we can feel lucky it did not turn into a global conflagration. We have Vladimir Putin to thank for that. Who else had the credibility in both Beijing and Washington to broker a cessation of hostilities? Regardless of what we think of

Putin's ways, no one would begrudge Russia's president the Nobel Peace Prize. But for Putin, we might now be picking through the smouldering ruins of World War Three. Come to think of it, Trump's cultivation of Putin looks to have been well ahead of its time. Moreover – and painful though it is to admit it – there may have been some method to Trump's madness. Though he stumbled recklessly into it, the US and China were probably destined for a showdown at some point. Most of us no longer seriously question that the world's future, and the fate of our values, will be settled in the struggle between a rising China and a hegemonic America. All else is embellishment and detail. Nurturing Putin's good offices – and coaxing Mother Russia into the arms of the Judeo-Christian West – seems in hindsight to have been a prescient strategy. We will endure whatever challenges today's hot peace with China may throw our way. If that means allowing Putin to take a slice of the Baltics, so be it. Almost half of Estonia's people speak Russian anyway. Putin may still be feted in Beijing. But we are essentially on the same side now.

How did we not see the wood from the trees? Reliving the build-up is a painful exercise. The fog of war is always thick. But it is fair to say Trump's administration was clear about its stance from the outset. The first big hint of an impending Sino-American showdown came at Rex Tillerson's confirmation hearings for Secretary of State in January 2017. He broke with long-standing policy on the contested South China Sea by saying the US would deny China access to the disputed

islands it claims – and on many of which it has built formida-
ble military installations. This was a big rupture in America's
position, which had maintained formal neutrality in the South
China Sea disputes but kept up freedom of navigation patrols
through the sea's international waters. Tillerson ripped all that
up. China's 'access to those islands is not going to be allowed',
he told senators. If necessary, the US Navy would interpose
itself between China and the islands. A few days later President
Trump formed his National Security Council. It would be
headed by Michael Flynn, the former general who co-authored
a 2016 book that accused China of being in cahoots with Isis.
Flynn was an unrepentant Sinophobe. He was also a fantasist.
Former Pentagon colleagues used to talk derisively of 'Flynn
facts',[2] which were his version of Trump's 'alternative facts'.
What was truly astonishing, however, was the inclusion of
Stephen Bannon in the NSC. Bannon's appointment as Trump's
senior political strategist had been troubling enough – the
former editor of Breitbart News is a self-declared Leninist who
wanted to 'blow the system up'. He would now have the right
to attend every NSC principals meeting. Yet the Director of
National Intelligence and the Chairman of the US Joint Chiefs
of Staff would only be included as and when they were needed.
Given Bannon's belief in the impending civilisational showdown
between the West and the rest, we should have drawn starker
conclusions.[3] The advice Trump would be getting on national
security would be dominated by men who saw China as the

enemy. Worse, it would often come unfiltered by the opinions of the heads of the Pentagon and US intelligence. It is hard to think of any US president who needed neutral advice more than Trump. The world was briefly reassured a month into Trump's term by his firing of Flynn (supposedly for having misled the vice-president, Mike Pence, on the nature of his conversations with the Russian ambassador) and his replacement with H. R. McMaster, a highly regarded general. But McMaster was no more able to curb his boss's impulses than the president himself. As a serving officer, he was also less inclined to.

The first rumblings came on trade. Three days before Trump's inaugural address, Xi Jinping reassured Davos that China did not wish to get into any trade wars. Shortly after swearing the oath of office, Trump said: 'We've made other countries rich, while the wealth, strength and confidence of our country has dissipated over the horizon ... Protection will lead to great prosperity and strength.' Guided by Peter Navarro, Trump's chief trade adviser, and author of *Death by China, How America lost its manufacturing base*, the US president gradually escalated measures against China, imposing steep anti-dumping duties on Chinese steel, semiconductors and engine parts. The WTO upheld China's complaints against America's actions. Trump promptly tweeted that he would ignore its rulings. 'The days of America selling its sovereignty to a rigged globalist body are over!' said Trump. 'America is in this to win #Greatagain'. Meanwhile, having fuelled a market boom with the biggest US tax cut in history, Trump fell out with the US Federal Reserve, which had embarked on a series of interest rate increases to curb the over-heating. Trump fired Janet Yellen and appointed Kevin Warsh, an inflation hawk turned dove, to replace her. Confidence in the dollar began to plummet. Sensing an opening, China unveiled a five-year roadmap to make the renminbi the world's co-equal premier reserve currency with the US dollar. Having exhausted the WTO option in 2017, China unveiled a series of retaliatory measures in mid-2018. 'We cannot sit passively while America sets fire to the global trading system,' said Xi. Though China made sure to calibrate its steps 'in proportion to the damage' the US had caused, there was little chance of turning back.

At what point did a hot war become inevitable? Some say it was when Trump ordered the Fifth Fleet to patrol just twelve miles from China's coastline – a technically permissible action, but highly provocative in the circumstances. Coming just three weeks before the 2018 mid-term elections, China's response to Trump's move – a flurry of intercontinental ballistic missile tests that reminded Americans that US cities were within easy reach of China's warheads – helped the Republicans retain control of Congress in spite of signs of a sharp economic slowdown. The GOP's election slogan, 'Standing strong against China', con-trasted strongly with the Democrats' 'True to America's values', which failed to paper over the party's growing disunity. Others date the point of no return to Trump's firing earlier that year of Jim Mattis, the Secretary of Defense, who strenuously objected to his exclusion from several key NSC meetings in which China was discussed. Though Mattis voiced his complaint privately, Trump fired him on Twitter. Mattis was replaced by Jeff Sessions, another China hawk, who had earned Trump's admiration as an iconoclastic Attorney General. With Mattis went one of the last big voices of caution. In reality, Mattis had long since forfeited Trump's trust by arguing against the resurrection of CIA-run black sites for Isis detainees. 'Circle of trust people!' tweeted Trump, just hours after firing Mattis.

In 2019, things began to spiral out of control. Buoyed by his mid-term victory, and backed by the swelling America First movement, Trump began the year with actions to demonstrate the middle classes were still at the heart of his agenda. In a flurry of executive orders, Trump announced the US would pull out of the WTO, stated that trading partners, such as China, would have to match their trade surpluses with US greenfield investments, and imposed a series of emergency tariffs on critical imports. Relations with China nosedived. Emboldened by Trump's aggression, Taiwan's president, Tsai Ing-Wen, announced in June that she would hold a referendum on independence in early 2020. Trump declared the US would stay neutral. China's reaction was swift and provocative. Putting its military forces on high alert, Beijing issued Taipei with an undated ultimatum: accept unification or face occupation. The following weeks were a maelstrom of confusion. Public order broke down in Taiwan as US carrier groups and Chinese naval patrols barely skirted each other in the Taiwan Strait. There were repeated near-misses in the skies. China's cities were brought to a halt by mass US flag-burning. Theresa May, Britain's prime minister, facing her own general election, was keen to take a break from post-Brexit UK to try to persuade Trump to moderate his offer to Taiwan. 'Whatever happened to the British bulldog?' tweeted Trump as May flew home empty-handed. Putin stayed publicly silent. China, meanwhile, dramatically escalated the stakes. Xi Jinping demanded the US withdraw its battle group from the Taiwan Strait or face the consequences. Trump's response was instant: 'America will never back down!' Hours later China's surface-to-air missile defence system shot down a US fighter plane that had strayed into Chinese airspace. Trump did not wait for the report. He ordered an instant salvo of punitive missile strikes on China's naval base on Hainan Island. Within an hour a Chinese nuclear submarine had torpedoed the USS *John McCain*. The world's two most powerful countries were on the cusp of nuclear war. Another escalation would have tipped it.

It was at that point Putin intervened. If truth be told, he was pushing at an open door. Sensing Armageddon, Beijing had pleaded for emergency diplomatic intervention even as the US destroyer was listing. Although Trump put US nuclear forces on final-stage alert, his Twitter account went eerily silent. Taipei, meanwhile, announced that it would be ready to open exploratory talks on the possible terms of Chinese unification. Trump would be welcomed as a friendly observer. China was prepared to go along with that. All Putin had to do was talk Trump down from the ledge. He was perhaps the only man on earth who could do so. There were at least a thousand Chinese dead, the Russian president observed, but only seventy-four Americans. 'My good friend Donald has shown the world that he will never back down from a fight,' said Putin, standing side by side with Trump on the White House lawn. 'Because of you, nobody questions America's greatness any more.' After another week of shuttle diplomacy, Putin presided over the signing ceremony in Moscow. The immediate crisis was over. Nobody was in much doubt that the US and China both ached with the wounds of unfinished business. At some point they would resume. Putin had negotiated a ceasefire, not a peace treaty. The world would not be the same. But we had avoided nuclear war. Moreover, most people now knew where they stood, even if many did so with deep misgivings. Theresa May congratulated Trump on showing real leadership. Trump, meanwhile, had rallied most of a badly polarised America to the flag. His approval ratings topped 60 per cent. The chances of a second term were rising. The days when America's foreign policy hawks casually mocked Trump's hold on reality were over. Most of them were falling into line.

A week before Neville Chamberlain boarded his infamous flight to Munich in 1938, John Maynard Keynes presented an unusual paper to his artsy friends in the Bloomsbury Group. The purpose of his reading, which he discharged languidly from a chaise longue, was to explore *My Early Beliefs*. Keynes possessed one of those rare intellects that perceived the connection between diverse fields.[4] He was a genius at numbers who worshipped aesthetics. He was a world-renowned scholar who navigated Whitehall's corridors of power. And he was an economist who grasped geopolitics better than its practitioners. At Versailles in 1919, where he served as an economic adviser, Keynes instantly realised that the post-war treaty had achieved the worst of both worlds. Versailles's terms would be too lenient to prevent a defeated Germany from recovering, yet they would be too punitive to allow for conciliation. In perceiving the *Economic consequences of the peace*, Keynes also foresaw its ominous geopolitical implications. His talk on the eve of the Second World War was about what the intervening decades had done to his early beliefs.

For an upper- or middle-class Englishman in the decade before the Great War, 'life offered, at a low cost and with the least trouble, conveniences, comforts, and amenities beyond the compass of the richest and most powerful monarchs of other ages,' Keynes had written in his Versailles monograph. Comfortable Edwardians regarded 'this state of affairs as normal, certain, and permanent, except in the direction of further improvement'. They were blissfully ignorant of what was about to hit them. As Keynes told the Bloomsbury circle almost twenty years later, 'We were not aware that civilization was a thin and precarious crust erected by the personality and the will of a very few, and only maintained by rules and conventions skilfully put across and guilefully preserved.' The Great War's industrial-scale slaughter, the incompetent and mean-spirited peace that followed, the collapse of the League of Nations, and the terrifying rise of a new Germany were by now all dreadfully familiar. How hard it was now to inhabit his pre-1914 mind – the Cambridge rationalist who, above all, had prized beauty, truth and the pursuit of knowledge, sailing obliviously into the war to end all wars. Looking back, Keynes saw himself and his generation as 'waterspiders, gracefully skimming, as light and reasonable as air, the surface of the stream without any contact at all with the eddies and currents underneath'.

Do we ever learn from history? If so, the parallels between the world today and the world in 1914 should strike us forcefully. Then, as now, the world's big economies were deeply intertwined. The decades preceding the First World War marked a peak of globalisation that the world economy only regained in the 1990s. Like today, people believed ever-deepening ties of commerce rendered the idea of war irrational. It was thus unthinkable. People had grown complacent after decades of peace. Of course, there was always the crackle of distant gunfire, such as Britain's Boer War, in South Africa, and periodic colonial skirmishes on almost every continent. But the last real clash between the 'civilised powers' had been more than forty years before, in the 1870–1 Franco-German War. Even then, it was strictly bilateral. Europe's last big war had wrapped up almost a century before, with Napoleon's defeat at Waterloo. Much like my own generation, someone of Keynes's age was unlikely to have direct experience of conflict – or any real fears they would be touched directly by war. Like the Boer War, the invasion of Iraq in 2003 took place in another time zone and was fought by a primarily lower-class volunteer army. The rest of us carried on shopping, as George W. Bush had urged us to do. More to the point, there was plenty of appetite to shop. Just as we exult in our Apple products and artisanal coffee, so Keynes's generation revelled in their Darjeeling tea and the internal combustion engine.

But the loudest echo is geopolitical. What struck Keynes's contemporaries as plain only in hindsight stands in full view before us today. Historians call it the Thucydides trap, after the Greek historian who chronicled Sparta's response to the rise of Athens. How does the established power react to the rise of a potential challenger? Should it pre-empt the possible threat or make accommodations to ensure it does not happen? Sparta opted for war with Athens and lost. A 2012 Harvard study examining fifteen such instances since 1500 found that in eleven cases the trap had culminated in war.[5] One example was the rise of Germany in the late nineteenth and early twentieth century. Victorian Britain was the hegemon; Bismarck's Germany the challenger. In 1880, Germany had barely a third of Britain's manufacturing production. By 1913, Germany had overtaken it.[6] The similarity to China and America today is unmissable. In 1970 China had just 3 per cent of global manufacturing. By the early 2000s it was producing more than the US. Not only has China risen as dizzily as Germany in the late nineteenth century, but it is also expanding its military capability at an equally unsettling speed. Once the undisputed ruler of the seas, Britain's navy went from virtual monopoly in the 'near waters' of Europe to parity with Germany in less than a generation. It still retained a big worldwide lead. But in Europe the two faced each other as near-equals. China, too, is fast developing a blue-water navy. More to the point, it now has sea-denial capacity in its neighbourhood. America's battle-carrier groups are no longer safe from China's submarine and anti-ship missile threats. China is capable of preventing America's continued military primacy in the Asia Pacific but it is not yet strong enough to supplant it. We are entering a period of radical uncertainty.

The trajectory was troubling even before Donald Trump was elected. It has been Washington's fixed view since the end of the Cold War that it will do whatever it takes to ensure America's enduring primacy in the Asia Pacific. This was as true of the Obama administration, whose 'pivot to Asia' was aimed at containing China, as of Bush and Clinton before that. But the means with which the US would achieve this have continually had to adjust to the breathtaking speed of China's rise. During the Clinton years, Washington's assumption was that a growing China could easily be hedged. The biggest moment came in 1996, after China conducted a series of missile tests in the Taiwan Strait. China launched the tests after America had invited Lee Teng-hui, Taiwan's president, to speak at Cornell University, which Beijing saw as an implicit weakening of America's One China policy. China also suspected that Lee harboured separatist sympathies. Clinton promptly ordered two aircraft carrier groups into the region, one of which, under the USS *Nimitz*, patrolled the Taiwan Strait. It worked. China backed off and Lee won a thumping re-election later that year. Yet Clinton's display of force also triggered unintended consequences. Drawing the obvious conclusions from its setback, China threw its energies into a military modernisation programme, buying ships and submarines from Russia and investing in a new generation of military technology. As a result, America today no longer wields undisputed sea control over China's neighbourhood. The power of a vast US aircraft carrier is little match for the stealth of a nuclear submarine, or the potency of China's anti-ship missiles. Clinton's manoeuvre would be a far more dramatic bet today. The risks of rapid escalation would be acute. China now has an aircraft carrier of its own – the *Liaoning* – and is building two more. 'People used to say that the carriers allowed America to project power without going to war,' says Hugh White, Australia's leading Sinologist. 'In future America will have to go to war before it can send in the carriers.'[7]

Bill Clinton also held another card that no longer looks like an ace – Washington's unshakeable faith in the march of history. As China developed, so its middle classes would demand greater freedom. Capitalism could not mature unless society gave free rein to the marketplace of ideas. All the West needed to do was draw China ever deeper into the global economy and the details would sort themselves out. In addition, technology would progressively liberate the growing Chinese middle class. As Jagdish Bhagwati, a leading trade economist, put it: 'the CP (the Communist Party) is not compatible with the PC [personal computer]'.[8] This was a big leap. In reality, the Washington Consensus badly misinterpreted the character of China's development. The better Beijing managed it, the more political kudos it earned. That, of course, is a double-edged sword: if growth slows, Beijing's political legitimacy may come into doubt. But that prospect was academic in the 1990s. China kept growing yet showed no signs of endorsing multi-party democracy. In late 2009, I travelled with Obama on his first trip to China. It was a sobering experience. Obama came offering China a G2 role as a co-manager with America of the world's main cross-border problems, notably climate change and terrorism. He also bore a familiar message: 'Prosperity without freedom is just another form of poverty,' Obama told his hosts. Obama's sermon clearly irritated Beijing, which went out of its way to humiliate him. Hu Jintao, China's then president, denied Obama's request to broadcast a student town-hall event on state television. Both Clinton and Bush had been allowed to do so. The Chinese also turned down Obama's request for a full press conference in the Great

Hall of the People. Scowling Public Security Bureau employees, smoking and unshaven, lounged disrespectfully outside Obama's hotel room in Shanghai. At the global-warming summit in Copenhagen a few weeks later, the Chinese pointedly refused to step up to the G2 role Obama had urged on them.

China's brush-off gave Obama a harsh tutorial in the ways of geopolitics. But he was a quick study. He unveiled his Asia pivot a year later. Though Obama was instinctively a realist, the Asia pivot was based on a fundamentally neoconservative worldview, which Hillary Clinton shared. If China clung to its autocratic path, it would pose a growing threat to others. By the same token, if it embraced a Western-style political system, it could be counted on to behave in a law-abiding way. The Asia pivot arose from the pessimistic view that China was showing no signs of democratising. From now on, the Pentagon would split its assets equally between the Atlantic region and the Asia Pacific region. America's global deployments had previously been distributed 60:40 in the Atlantic's favour. The US would open new bases in Darwin, Australia, and the Philippines. Washington would also take a more robust stand on the disputed islands in the South China Sea – what Beijing calls the first island chain. Obama adopted a zero-sum position that set the US and China on a collision course. America would be committed to resolving the sovereignty dispute through international law. China would be just as committed to enforcing its unilateral claims to the islands. Each position has only hardened. Neither can back down without tremendous loss of face. If the US accepted Beijing's claims it would essentially be conceding regional primacy to China. If China accepted US-imposed arbitration, it would be submitting to continued American hegemony. It is hard, if not impossible, to imagine either country stepping down. Rex Tillerson has raised the stakes even further. The coming years will pit Trump's *The Art of the Deal* against Sun Tzu's *The Art of War*. There can be little doubt which approach is wilier. My US–China war scenario was triggered by just one of a deepening thicket of Sino-American trip-wires.

The chances that Trump will casually threaten China and get pulled into a dynamic he cannot control should be taken very seriously. Bismarck once said, 'Preventive war is like committing suicide out of fear of death.' It is conceivable Trump is possessed by some kind of morbid spirit. More worrying, however, is his proudly held ignorance of how other countries think – and thus how rivals such as China will interpret his actions. As Sun Tzu, Carl von Clausewitz and others observed in earlier times, the key to good diplomacy is to put yourself in your opponent's shoes. Reducing the scope for confusion is the best way to prevent wars. Even Trump's vastly better-informed predecessors found it hard to see the world from China's point of view. It is a difficult habit to shake. The West in general has imposed its preoccupations on China for more than two hundred years. From Hegel to John Stuart Mill, our greatest philosophers unanimously wrote off China as a lost cause to modernity. Each of them had different reasons. Hegel and then Marx dismissed China as an oriental despotism. Mill saw it as a flawed civilisation. Social Darwinians classified the Chinese as belonging to the lower races. Max Weber said Confucian culture would forestall the rise of capitalism since it had no conception of life after death. Is it worth adding that none of these thinkers set foot in China?[9]

Each of these precepts, some of them highly eccentric, has been belied by China's rise. 'The pamphlets and treatises of the colonial powers from the dawn of the twentieth century reveal a remarkable arrogance, to the effect that they were entitled to shape a world order by their maxims,' writes Henry Kissinger, who is well acquainted with China.[10] Yet we keep replacing one flawed prognosis with another. In the 1990s, Paul Krugman, the Nobel Prize-winning economist, wrote off the 'Asian growth miracle' as a mirage. Asia's economies were simply mobilising resources, much as the Soviet Union had done. Their model would go the same way as Stalin's.[11] Our most recent forecast – that China is on a one-way track to democracy – is faring little better. What strikes Westerners (and I am no exception) as self-evidently a good thing sounds to Chinese ears just another example of missionary zeal. There is a 'deeply held unconscious assumption that the West remains, in one way or another, a morally superior civilization,' writes Kishore Mahbubani, one of Singapore's foremost foreign policy thinkers.[12]

The secret to any nation's diplomatic character is embedded

in its popular imagination. If asked which historic events made them proudest, most British would choose the darkest days of the Second World War, when Britain faced Nazi Germany alone. Many would also mention the defeat of the Spanish Armada in the reign of Elizabeth I, or victory over Napoleon. Britain's worst fears, and deepest triumphs, have always coincided with Europe's unification under one power. The past is never really dead. It is not even past. The 2016 Brexit vote was today's version of Henry VIII's break with Rome. Most Americans would probably point to the defeat of the Axis Powers in the Second World War and victory over the Soviet Union in the Cold War. Many would also mention the US Constitution. Others would cite the landing of the first humans on the moon. Or perhaps the internet. Each instance reflects America's deep-seated belief in its own freedoms – and spreading them to others. Think of Jefferson's Empire of Liberty and George W. Bush's Freedom Agenda. What makes Chinese proud? I asked Eric Li, the Shanghai-based private equity investor, which two historic events he prized above others. The first was China's detonation of the hydrogen bomb in October 1964. This proved the Chinese people had 'stood up', as Mao promised in 1949. 'It was so extraordinary because the People's Republic was just fifteen years old and very poor,' said Li.[13] The test also proved China was capable of catching up with Western technology. The second was Britain's transfer of Hong Kong to China in 1997. The handover 'closed the curtain on China's "century of humiliation" at the hands of foreign invaders'. Both of Li's examples show China's deep-rooted desire to be treated with respect and dignity.

Alas, the West keeps shifting the goal posts. It was only in the early 1990s, several years after the Sino-British deal on Hong Kong, that the UK introduced a modest amount of representative democracy to the city state. The Hong Kong legislative council's new powers were little match for those of the London-appointed governor. Partly, it is a matter of tone. The one country, two systems framework to which China agreed is far more democratic than anything the UK granted to Hong Kong. Yet even today, British Members of Parliament noisily protest when China fails to live up to the letter of its democratic promises. It is as though Manchu China had only just returned the Channel Islands to Britain after seizing them in the nineteenth century, then spent the next twenty years hectoring the UK about how it should govern them. China can easily brush aside Britain's double standards: London, in any case, is switching to a more mercantilist stance in which it now rolls out the red carpet for China. America is a different matter. So, too, is Taiwan. China's incentive to maintain Hong Kong's relative freedoms has less to do with honouring its obligations to Britain than with convincing Taiwan that its way of life would be secure under China's rule. Taiwan is the big prize. Washington is the biggest obstacle. It is critical to try to see the dispute from China's point of view. Since Washington proclaimed the Monroe Doctrine in 1823, the US has treated outside interference in the Western hemisphere as a threat to its national interests. That includes Cuba, which the US helped liberate from Spanish colonial rule in 1898. The Caribbean island never fell under US sovereignty. Yet John F. Kennedy was prepared to risk nuclear war with the Soviets over the transfer of Soviet missiles to Cuba. In contrast, Taiwan was not only an historic part of China, but is recognised as such by the US and most of the rest of the world. It split off from the mainland only in 1949, after the defeated Kuomintang fled there following the communist revolution. Taiwan was shielded from Mao's wrath by America. Today, US nuclear-armed warships regularly patrol twelve miles from China's shores. What would happen if China's nuclear-equipped warships were spotted off the coast of Virginia? How would Washington respond if Chinese drones took out separatist exiles in, say, Central America, or even Central Asia? Not calmly, it can be safely assumed.

Until Trump, Washington could still just about argue that only the US could be trusted to play the role of global policeman. As an autocracy without allies, China lacked the basic means to uphold the global commons. Bush Junior's pre-emptive wars badly damaged America's unipolar credentials. Trump's victory has smashed them to pieces. It is questionable whether Humpty Dumpty can be put together again. A more serious question is whether China would aspire to play such a role, even if it could somehow convince the rest of the world to go along with it. China's history casts a lot of doubt on that theory. In the early fifteenth century, almost ninety years before Christopher Columbus set sail for the New World, China assembled the largest naval fleet then known to history under the admiralship of Zheng He. The fleet took several trips south and west, ranging as far as the mouth of the Red Sea and down Africa's eastern coastline. Yet it set up no colonies along the way. On Zheng's final voyage he dropped off the foreign envoys he had picked up on the earlier trips. Even at the height of its imperial power, China preferred to diffuse its culture through osmosis rather than by conquest. As Kissinger points out, both the US and China see themselves as exceptional.[14] But China's version of exceptionalism is unique to itself. Others were encouraged to copy China's culture and pay tribute. Those who refused to do so were treated as barbarians and slapped into line. But China has rarely sought to export its model by force or colonise other lands. The last time China disciplined a recalcitrant was in 1979, when the People's Liberation Army crossed the border into Vietnam and gave it a bloody nose. China then promptly withdrew. Prior to that was the Sino-Indian war of 1962, in which Chinese forces overran Indian resistance but halted once they reached the line Beijing claimed was the correct border. It was less a war to put India in its place than a war to rectify China's century of humiliation: the British had shifted India's border eastwards in the nineteenth century, at a moment of Chinese weakness. Today, Taiwan remains by far China's largest item of unfinished business. Only the US stands in its way. Under Trump, the two great countries seem almost destined to stray into some kind of crisis.

Suppose Donald Trump took a magic pill that gave him a sudden thirst for knowledge. How would that change his view of the world? First, he would cherish and nurture America's allies, instead of accusing them of being free-riders. It makes no sense to take a belligerent approach to China while insulting its neighbours. He would also try to put himself in their shoes. That would mean firing Peter Navarro and reviving the Trans-Pacific Trade Partnership, which includes Japan, South Korea, Vietnam, Australia and six other countries – but not China. Instead, Trump has chosen to drive America's regional allies into China's arms. Even Australia, which comes closest to US values, wants to enter China's rival trade group, the Regional Comprehensive Economic Partnership. Post-pill Trump would also reassure Japan that it would remain a close ally of America under its nuclear umbrella. The more secure Japan feels, the less likely it is to develop its own nuclear capability – a feat it could pull off in a matter of months. He would also pay far closer attention to India, the only country in Asia that could possibly act as a counterbalance to China. After taking a second pill, Trump would also grasp the logic of building closer relations with China. The old mindset dictates that you cannot move closer to China and Japan at the same time. Pre-pill Trump believes you can alienate both simultaneously. The new mindset would transcend that binary worldview. The US would neither withdraw from Asia, nor insist on its absolute primacy. Instead, it would promote a regional balance of power with the US as the swing vote. Post-pill Trump would also go out of his way to reassure China that America viewed military conflict as a disaster in which no one could possibly emerge the winner. He would also encourage Taiwan to open its own one country, two systems negotiations. Taiwan's importance to China dramatically outweighs any US stake in the island's status. It would be madness to risk global stability over it.

Having digested China's worldview, Trump would also understand how worried Beijing was about its own internal stability. Fear of Chinese domination would be replaced with worry about its collapse. As China's growth slows, and the seventieth anniversary of its revolution looms, Xi Jinping will be tempted to shore up his support with nationalist diversions. He will probably also tighten his crackdown on internal dissent. The longest-lasting revolutionary state in history ended after seventy-four years with the Soviet Union's demise. Xi Jinping's presidential term is scheduled to end in 2022, precisely seventy-three years after China's revolution. It would be a disaster if Xi broke with Chinese precedent and prolonged his hold on power. The country could break up into a new era of warring states, which would push the world into recession and destabilise Asia. For what it is worth, I think a China break-up is very unlikely. But China has been unified for less than half of its 2200-year history. Just as America fears ideological competition, and Britain has historically dreaded a unified continent, so China is constantly paranoid about internal dissolution. The better Trump understood Xi's qualms, the more he would be able to assuage them. Finally, Trump would learn how to say hello in Mandarin. A little bit of effort goes a long way.

Alas, no such pill exists. Even if it did, Trump would probably refuse to take it. Trump's animating spirit is to make a demoralised American middle class feel better about itself. His goal is to channel rage, not cultivate knowledge. In so doing, he has licence to indulge his most authoritarian impulses. China is the most obvious external target. But it is a scapegoat, not a culprit. China's labour force is subject to precisely the same forces of automation as its American counterparts – and suffers from even greater inequality. The potential for a populist backlash in China cannot be overlooked. Theoretically, the US still has more leverage than any other country in shaping the future character of a multipolar world. But Trump is rapidly squandering America's fund of goodwill. Within days of his inauguration Trump had killed the remaining spirit of enlightened self-interest that defined much of post-war America. Churchill described America's Lend-Lease aid to Britain in the early part of the Second World War as the 'most unsordid act in history'. At best, Trump is shaping up to be the most sordid leader America has produced. At worst he could blunder into war with China, and spark a war of all against all in the Middle

East. Trump is too narcissistic to change for the better. The stability of the planet – and the presumption of restraint – will have to rest in the hands of Xi Jinping and other powerful leaders. To forestall disaster, the rest of the world will have no choice but to try to put themselves in Trump's shoes. We all have need of that magic pill now.

———————

Populist nationalism is staging a comeback just as global cooperation is most desperately needed. There has been a lot of focus on America's decline – I even wrote a book on the subject: *Time to Start Thinking: America and the Spectre of Decline* (2012). America's relative decline is real. But the larger picture is even more troubling. Governments of all types – democratic and authoritarian, small states and superpowers – are losing their ability to anticipate events. They are thus losing the means to shape them. The days when national leaders could peer around the corner and head off coming dangers are receding. The best foreign policy is conducted by calm minds in possession of the facts – and shielded from the pressure to broadcast instant moral absolutes. The more time leaders have to weigh up their options the likelier they are to choose the right ones. The speed of technological change is working against them. It is a tragedy that democracy is on the retreat at this time. At some level, most of us believe that autocracies are more efficient than democracies. It is a myth. During the Second

World War, the two most efficient belligerents by far were the US and Britain. Even during the bleakest parts of the war there was no question of suspending most forms of political freedom.[15] The degree of public trust in both countries enabled their wartime governments to commandeer resources and direct them to a common end, through voluntary means rather than by coercion. By contrast, Hitler and Stalin squandered huge resources and strategic intelligence by setting their key henchmen against each other. The paranoia of strongmen far outweighs the supposed efficiency of their methods. Trust is the glue of a successful free society; fear is the currency of the autocrat. It is the former that is most desperately needed. By this measure – the most important of all – Trump is an unabashed autocrat. The more resistance he encounters, the more he will sow mistrust. Technology is Trump's friend. Science is his enemy.

The first great modern age of science found its counterpart in the relationship between states. The Peace of Westphalia, which was born in 1648, set in motion a new system in which each state could choose its own confessional character, Protestant or Catholic. Each also pledged to respect the internal character of other states while respecting the rights of their religious minorities. Westphalia brought an end to the Hobbesian war of all against all that had reduced Europe to cinders. It set up a diplomatic mechanism that could be likened to Newton's laws of physics.[16] The same principle underlay the post-Napoleonic Concert of Europe that kept the peace for almost a century. States did not interfere in one another's internal politics. As Bismarck's Germany rose and upset the equilibrium, Newtonian physics made way for a Darwinian survival of the fittest. Biology replaced mechanics and gave rise to the two most genocidal wars in our history.

What science fits the twenty-first-century world? By today's standards, it would be feat enough if we could return to some kind of Westphalian order. But the forces working against stability are too overwhelming to imagine we can reverse the clock. Rising disorder, the growing randomness of events and the exponential rate of technological change are making erratic particles of us all. We are moving into a Brownian world. The *Oxford English Dictionary*'s definition of Brownian movement is 'the irregular oscillatory movement observed in microscopic particles or "molecules" of all kinds suspended in a limpid fluid; also called *molecular movement*'. This also describes our digital age. The surge of bytes in a networked world favours cyber-chaos. In short, we are entering a period where instability is growing and the centre will struggle to hold.

In writing *Nothing Is True and Everything Is Possible*, one of the books that best captures the spirit of our times, Peter Pomerantsev got to know Vladimir Putin's right-hand man, Vladislav Surkov. A self-described political technologist, Surkov fashioned the tools Putin uses to divert attention, sow confusion and level the playing field between truth and lies. Surkov is something of an evil genius: he understands that human weaknesses – the capacity to be diverted and the yearning to be relieved from boredom – are putty in the hands of a technological maestro. In the late Soviet era, no one believed in communism any more but they were forced to carry on their lives as if they did. Now they live in a society of simulations in which the pretence of democracy has replaced that old set of beliefs. Surkov also writes fiction under the pen name Natan Dubovitsky. Egor, the anti-hero of his novel *Almost Zero*, is a sort of '"vulgar Hamlet" who can see through the superficiality of his age but is unable to have genuine feelings for anyone or anything'. Shortly before Putin annexed Crimea in 2014, Surkov/Dubovitsky published a short story called 'Without Sky'. It is set in the near future following the 'fifth world war, the first non-linear war of all against all'. Nobody really knows whose side they are on, who is waging the war, and for what. 'In the primitive wars of the nineteenth and twentieth centuries it was common for just two sides to fight,' writes Surkov. 'Two countries, two blocks of allies. Now four coalitions collided. Not two against two, or three against one. All against all.' Those who profit the most are those best able to exploit the forces of chaos rather than work against them. Putin is the exemplar. His use of information warfare and psychological operations in Crimea created enough of a myopia to wrong-foot the Ukrainians. Nothing was true. Everything was deniable. Trump is a student of Putin's ways. He believes the system is rigged. Stephen Bannon, who wants to 'blow the system up', is emerging as Trump's Surkov.

The world is sailing into a fog that Keynes would recognise as radical uncertainty. Nationalism is returning at the same time as technology is obliterating walls between nations. No amount of bricks and mortar, or cybernetic Maginot Lines, can stop its flow. This is creating two existential challenges for the world in the years ahead. The first is changing the nature of relations between nations. The second is an upheaval in the internal character of states. Each feeds off and reinforces the other. The biggest duty of any state is to protect the nation from enemies. In the pre-nuclear age, this was accomplished with large-scale armies. During the nuclear era, it moved increasingly to weapons of mass destruction. Although the Cold War involved near-misses, most notably during the Cuban Missile Crisis of 1962, the Americans and the Soviets gradually came to understand each other's signals. Eventually each was able to read the other's nuclear grammar fluently. After 1962 the two sides set up a nuclear hotline and even agreed to exchanges of personnel so that they could minimise the risk they would stumble into war. The doctrine of mutually assured destruction worked because it was based on an understanding between two highly organised actors. Russia and the United States have both cut their stockpiles of nuclear weapons drastically since the end of the Cold War. Today their arsenals stand at roughly a tenth of where they were at their peak.

Yet today's nuclear world is far more dangerous than during the Cold War. Instead of having five nuclear weapons states – the permanent members of the United Nations Security Council (the USSR, the US, France, China and the UK) – the world now has nine. Israel, India, Pakistan and North Korea have joined the club. That tally could ratchet up to fifteen in fairly short order. The barriers to nuclear entry keep falling. Countries that are considered capable of carrying out a rapid nuclear breakout include Japan, Egypt, Australia, Turkey, Saudi Arabia and Iran. Moreover, the two big nuclear weapons states, Russia and America, are no longer so intimate with each other's nuclear protocols. The trust has gone. Under Putin, Russia is far less of a responsible nuclear custodian than it was during the post-Cuba decades. Meanwhile, China and India are both in the midst of their own undeclared arms race: China's nuclear deterrent is mostly targeted at the US; India's is mostly aimed at countering Pakistan. Pakistan, which operated its own nuclear Walmart under the notorious A. Q. Khan in the 1990s, enabling North Korea to launch its programme, is also rapidly modernising its arsenal. In the age of Trump, the spectre of rapid nuclear proliferation is greater than at any time since nuclear weapons were invented.

Nuclear control is a fundamentally top-down problem. It cannot be solved by civil society. Without American participation it will never happen. Barack Obama tried his best. I was in Prague with Obama in 2009 when he made his famous speech calling for a world of zero nuclear weapons.[17] It was a laudable goal, though he did not get very far. But he bravely declared it to be urgent and made an effort to launch a global dialogue. Donald Trump has expressed no interest in the subject. Before taking office, his knowledge of nuclear weapons was worse than rudimentary. During one of the presidential debates, Trump made it clear that he had no idea what the nuclear triad meant (launch capabilities from air, land and sea). He is also the first US president to have openly speculated about using them. 'Somebody hits us within Isis – you wouldn't fight back with a nuke?' he said in one campaign interview.[18] While Trump is president, global proliferation is almost certain to get worse. Indeed, he has expressly called for a new nuclear arms race. '[If] countries are going to have nukes, we are going to be top of the pack,' he said shortly after becoming president.[19]

Just as we believed history had come to an end, so we thought we had entered a post-nuclear age. On the contrary, the risk of nuclear conflict has never been higher. The threat of cyber war has since been added to the equation. It poses the opposite problem to Cold War bilateral deterrence. Cyber weapons are the ultimate in asymmetric warfare. Not only are they at the disposal of multiple players – countless players, if you include non-state actors – but it is often impossible to know who is hitting you. Was that a branch of the Kremlin, or a rogue Russian operative? Was that an outfit of the People's Liberation Army or a bunch of nihilistic hackers? Was it Isis, or Iran? If you do not know who is attacking you, or who is likely to attack you next, how is it possible to deter them with the threat of retaliation?

Even when you can identify your assailant, it is hard to know what kind of counter-attack is appropriate. Does a virtual attack merit a kinetic response? Suppose there was a cyber-attack on US air traffic control that caused a mid-air collision, with hundreds of casualties. Or an electric grid outage that caused a surge in mortality. Suppose also that you knew the identity of the attacker. Would a military response be merited? If not, why not? If so, where do you stop? The line between reality and virtual reality is blurring. Some of America's best strategists have been working on the problem for almost a decade. They have yet to come up with a clear doctrine. Mutually assured destruction does not work, yet nothing has emerged to take its place. The US Cyber Command believes the next global war will start in cyberspace. Doubtless they are talking up their own book. But they are right to worry that the temptation to strike by stealth is irresistible on a battlefield in which there are no rules of engagement. Nor are there any limits to the battlefield. '[Because] of the seamless worldwide network, the packets, and the Internet of Things, cyber war [will] involve not just soldiers, sailors, and pilots but, inexorably, the rest of us,' says Fred Kaplan, author of *Dark Territory: The Secret History of Cyber War.* 'When cyberspace is everywhere, cyber war can seep through every digital pore.' The good news about cyber warfare is that it can never rival the damage caused by nuclear weapons. The bad news is that it is a permanent war.

When Pentagon meetings turned to cyber war, Bob Gates,

America's former Defense Secretary, would mutter, 'We are entering dark territory again'.[20] It was a phrase used by his grandfather, who worked on the railways, about the stretches of line where there were no signals. It is a good description of the networked world.

They say the first casualty of war is truth. In cyber war, truth is a primary target. States, such as Russia, and non-state entities, such as Isis, can generate fake stories at will and make them look as though they came from elsewhere. The system will do the rest. In 2016, a huge number of fake news stories were picked up via Facebook. That year was also a record one for Facebook advertising revenues. It would be expecting a lot of America's third-largest company to kill such a large source of its revenue growth – even assuming it could develop an algorithm that sifted true from false. When confusion is a strategic goal, it is doubly important for public figures to have the credibility to refute dangerous inaccuracies. Indeed, it is a matter of national security. It goes without saying that Donald Trump lacks any such trust. He is far more likely to be a source of wild propaganda than a check on it. Three days after Trump was sworn in, he personally telephoned the head of the US National Park Service to ask him to remove a tweet that showed unfavourable photos of the thin crowds at Trump's inauguration versus the overflow at Barack Obama's. The tweet was promptly taken down. The next time a US public official considers putting out information that may show Trump in a bad light, they will think twice. Trump's White House team has publicly told US diplomats to resign rather than express misgivings through the State Department's long-standing dissent channel, which permits diplomats to voice concerns anonymously. It is an important outlet for internal discussion.

There is no such thing as neutral information. For populists, facts are either with them or against them. The war against truth is now being waged from the White House. Trump has made it clear the post-war US-led global order is history. But what will replace it? Some fear that China is the coming power. But chaos, not China, is likelier to take America's place. At Trump's encouragement, America's network of alliances is now starting to unravel. In Britain, which was post-war America's closest ally, there was a saying that the aim was to keep the Germans down, the Americans in, and the Russians out. All three are now failing. Putin's Russia has gained a toehold in many central European democracies, and increasingly in Western Europe. Some have likened him to a corporate raider, who buys a minority share of a company's stock and uses his voting power to disrupt the company. His goal is European disunity. It is an aim he shares with Trump. America's forty-fifth president has called for other members of the European Union to follow Britain's lead. After taking office, Trump publicly enquired which European country would be the next to make an exit. Trump has also continued to cast doubt on the future of Nato. Finally Germany is rising, but Trump wants to cut it down. He described Angela Merkel's decision to allow in Syrian refugees as a disaster. Peter Navarro declared Germany a currency manipulator and an unfair trader.[21] Merkel is now the only European leader with any serious presence on the global stage. The spirit of Western internationalism rests on her shoulders. It is asking a lot of a fourth-term German leader to carry such a torch. As Russia steps up its interference in Europe, Germany will be tempted to re-emerge as a military power. That would sure terrify the ghosts of history. But where else can we look? When Merkel had to postpone her first meeting with Trump due to snow, Brookings's Thomas Wright tweeted, 'Meeting between the leader of the free world and the President of the United States postponed till Friday.' He was only half-joking. Yet Germany's burden may be too great. Can Merkel uphold sanctions on Russia if America turns against them? Will she permit the European periphery to grow? Can she contain Europe's immigration crisis?

This book does not dare offer precise forecasts. But it is safe to say that if Germany fails to lead Europe, the European Union will fall apart. Europe may have to turn into a fortress in order to save itself. Even before Merkel allowed in up to a million Syrian refugees, global migration had hit a post-war peak. Three per cent of the world's population now live in countries other than where they were born. According to Gallup surveys of global migration, 16 per cent of the world – 700 million people – would move to wealthier nations if they could.[22] This is especially true of Africa and the Middle East. Many more will keep trying. For reasons of geography, Europe is their natural destination. That is even more true now that Trump is US president. His temporary visa ban on arrivals from six Muslim nations looks likely to be expanded once he overcomes the legal barriers. Which means even more refugees and economic migrants will be heading to Europe. European democracy cannot survive another decade like the last. Populism almost always offers a cure worse than the disease. But Hungary's Viktor Orbán was right about one thing: Europe should have secured its external border before it scrapped its internal ones. The free movement of peoples is now threatened by the populist backlash against the dramatic increase of outside arrivals. The amount of money spent on Frontex, Europe's fledgling border agency, is a fraction of what it needs to police the borders. Tough though it sounds, Europe cannot solve the Middle East by importing it. Nor does it have the capacity to absorb millions of Africa's economic migrants. Europe needs to make extremely difficult trade-offs to save itself.

Within days of taking office, Trump's America had already made those trade-offs dramatically worse. Fukuyama's 'The End of History?' may be wrong. But that does not mean Samuel Huntington's *The Clash of Civilizations* must be proved right. Trump's barely disguised targeting of Muslims vindicates the apocalyptic worldview of groups like Isis, which tell Muslims the West is at war with Islam. Now they have solid evidence. Stephen Bannon's vision of a Judeo-Christian world in mortal combat with Islam is a gift to radicals everywhere. It offers the mirror image of a sectarian West to a sectarian Middle East. Extreme vetting is becoming the leitmotif of post-2016 America. The fact that Trump's main targets are themselves victims of terrorism, rather than the perpetrators, is irrelevant. The action was inherently political. Its audience is American. Opponents of Trump's visa ban argue that the order omitted countries, such as Saudi Arabia, that supplied the 9/11 attackers. Moreover, the vast majority of domestic terrorist attacks since then have been carried out by US-born Muslims, many of them recent converts to Islam. Such critiques are sadly quixotic. They assume Trump's aim is to improve US security. But it was Bannon who drew up Trump's first botched executive order, not the security experts. Bannon's agenda is civilisational: his language reveals that. Even Putin, who leads a federation that is almost a fifth Muslim, takes great pains to avoid tarring a world religion with that brush. 'I would prefer Islam not be mentioned in vain alongside terrorism,' said Putin in a press conference in December 2016. Putin invariably refers to Isis as the 'so-called Islamic state'.[23] His vocabulary never wavers. George W. Bush, who visited Washington's Islamic Center six days after 9/11 to reassure Muslims there was no war on their religion, never faltered from that distinction either. Nor did Obama. But in the eyes of the Islamists, Trump has simply dropped the pretence. The West was always at war with Islam. Trump has removed the mask. At a moment when Isis is on the military retreat in Iraq and Syria,

Trump has made their drive for fresh recruits much easier. What will Trump do when the first domestic terrorist attack happens on his watch? The massacre in San Bernardino took place in late 2015, just as Trump's primary campaign was consolidating its lead. That was when Trump first proposed the Muslim visa ban. He also talked of setting up a national Muslim database, which would have chilling implications for US equality before the law. Setting up a registry of American Muslims would almost certainly be unconstitutional, whoever drafted the language. But the law takes its time. The damage would be incalculable.

For better or for worse – and I believe mostly for the better – America's democracy has been linked to its foreign policy for more than seventy years. Even where it proved hypocritical, such as in the 'war on terror' and during much of the Cold War, the idea of America proved greater than its faults. The link between an America that upheld its system at home and promoted it abroad was never broken, though often tarnished. Trump is inverting that link. The more scorn he pours on democratic traditions at home, the more he endangers them abroad. The Middle East is perhaps the most combustible laboratory. It will require a lot more tenacity for Arabs to make the case for democracy in the post-2016 world than before – and that is saying something. The same applies to the Chinese, Russians, Africans and people everywhere. The crisis of Western democracy is also a crisis of international relations. They are two sides of the same coin. Western liberal democracy is not yet dead, but it is far closer to collapse than we may wish to believe. It is facing its gravest challenge since the Second World War. This time, however, we have conjured up the enemy from within. At home and abroad, America's best liberal traditions are under assault from its own president. We have put arsonists in charge of the fire brigade. The bad news is that populists such as Donald Trump and Nigel Farage are winning the fight. The good news is that the fightback has a lot of room for improvement.

PART FOUR

HALF LIFE

Forgiveness is the key to action and freedom.

HANNAH ARENDT

'That is not who we are.' From the district councillor to Barack Obama, I have lost count of how many times I have heard that phrase. It is usually meant with very good intentions. When a nation is reeling from an elementary-school massacre, it needs reassurance. What just occurred was an aberration – it is not who we are. Yet the sentiment has been devalued by rampant inflation. Electing Mitt Romney in 2012 would have gone against who we are. Ditto for building a wall, backing capital punishment or opposing gay marriage. For what it is worth, I strongly support marriage equality and dread gun culture. But the words betray an incorrigible tendency to present the latest shift in liberal thinking as self-evident truth. The most surprising example of this was Obama's 2016 order threatening to withhold funds from schools that denied children their choice of gender identity. Critics labelled those who opposed the bathroom rule transphobes. Whatever right is in dispute, those who oppose it are invariably told they are on the wrong side of history – another frequent Obamaism. Such language is open to two criticisms. First, it reinvents the past. For example, Obama himself did not support gay marriage until he was nearly four years into his presidency.[1] Hillary Clinton waited until 2013. That was not who they were until recently, in other words. Was the truth not self-evident until then? Before the trans-gender bathroom issue arose, I doubt that either had spared it a moment's thought. Second, the moral tone almost always boom-erangs. People feel patronised. If your opponents are not who we are, where does that leave them? Presumably they are on the wrong side of history, which is not a place anybody wants to be. If politics is persuasion, these are dangerous tactics. There is a thin line between convincing people of the merits of a case and suggesting they are moral outcasts if they fail to see it. Liberal America crossed that line long before Obama took office.

Some time during the 1960s, the Western left abandoned the politics of solidarity to embrace one of personal liberation. You can pick your moment. Philip Larkin, the misanthropic English poet, traced Britain's cultural shift to the early 1960s: 'Sexual intercourse began / In nineteen sixty-three … Between the end of the "Chatterley" ban / And the Beatles' first LP.' Larkin's style and imagery were flippant, but he called the decade. More seriously, many in France would date the switchover to the mass student protests that paralysed Paris in 1968. Though somewhat arbitrary, my preferred American moment was the battle between student anti-war protesters and the Chicago police at the 1968 Democratic Convention.[2] In *Miami and the Siege of Chicago*, Norman Mailer described what happens when a party's base severs from its leadership. Inside the besieged hall, party brokers fixed the nomination of Hubert Humphrey, the unpopular vice-president who backed the Vietnam War. Outside, mayor Richard Daley's cops beat up the protesting hippies. '[The] Democratic Party had here broken in two before the eyes of a nation like Melville's whale charging right out of the sea,' wrote Mailer. The protesters' platform called for the abolition of money, disarmament of the police and full *un*employment. Daley's largely Irish and Italian working-class police came off the better in the violent battles that ensued. But the hippies won the war. In 1972 the McGovern–Fraser Commission changed the party's course. It included obligatory seats for women, ethnic minorities and young people – but left out working males altogether. 'We aren't going to let these Camelot Harvard-Berkeley types take over our party,' said the head of the AFL-CIO, the largest American union federation.[3] That is exactly what happened.

Starting with Reagan Democrats, and later Bush Republicans, blue-collar whites gradually moved over to the conservative banner. It took them a long time to feel buyer's remorse. Much the same happened in Britain when the skilled working classes broke away from Labour to vote Conservative in 1979. They were key to Margaret Thatcher's electoral success, and now form the backbone of UKIP. Republicans have spent the last forty years stoking white anxiety while ignoring the white working classes' economic insecurities – or making them worse. They used the dog whistle to channel resentments against multiculturalism. Then along came Trump with his megaphone. The rest is history, as they say. But who is on its right side? Does history's long arc bend towards justice, as Obama so poetically laid out? Is progress built 'one brick at a time, calloused hand by calloused hand'?[4] That is surely so. Reform is the fruit of painstaking effort. The civil rights victories of the 1960s were won by courageous people who were prepared to risk their lives. But I have grave doubts about history's long arc. History is not some self-driving car taking humanity to a pre-set destination. Whichever human is behind the wheel must ensure the others stay in the car. Telling some of the passengers they have no business in the driver's seat because they are clueless about the destination will sooner or later result in a crash. 'Take back control' was the chant of Brexiteers and Trump voters alike. It is the war cry of populist backlashes across the Western world.

There are two ways of deciphering that impulse. One is to dismiss it as the last reaction of the bigots, who wish to turn the clock back on two generations of hard-won rights for women and ethnic and sexual minorities. These are the people who 'cling to guns or religion or antipathy to people who aren't like them', as Obama said in 2008. Another is to listen to what they say. Some of their anxieties are cultural. Others are economic.

The debate over which of the two is fuelling the backlash is irresolvable: they are braided together. If we write off half of society as deplorable we forfeit claims on their attention. We also endanger liberal democracy. It is one thing to persuade ourselves that we know the future. It is another to miss what is happening in front of our eyes. Since the late 1970s, Western governments of right and left have been privatising risk. To one degree or another – most sharply in the US and the UK – societies are creeping back to the days before social insurance. What was once underwritten by government and employers has been shifted to the individual. When people hit the buffers, they knew there were funds to tide them over. Those guarantees have been relentlessly whittled down. The retreat of the state has coincided with a revolution in the nature of work. More and more jobs are piecemeal, outsourced and temporary. People are increasingly responsible for providing their own pensions and maintaining their workplace skills. In Britain, the move towards zero hours, in which the employee has no say over how long they can work, has metastasised. Almost 60 per cent of the US labour force are now paid hourly wages rather than annual incomes.[5] The median hourly wage is $15.61. The working class has moved from making stuff to serving people. Most of America's truck drivers are now independent contractors. They are known as sharecroppers on wheels.[6]

Regardless of where history places them, these people are on the wrong side of the economy. But it is not the sum total of who they are. Our tidy minds shunt all such trends into the economic silo. If only we could raise the minimum wage, or offer portable benefits to gig workers, we would fix the problem. But that is to miss the grander social dimension of what is happening. If you listen to what people are saying you get a much more troubling picture of the depth of post-modern anxiety. In survey after survey, the biggest employee complaint is being treated with a lack of respect.[7] Whether they work in an Amazon warehouse, serve fast food, or sit in a BT customer-service cubicle, they feel diminished by how they are treated. People must request permission for bathroom breaks from supervisors who are clocking every minute of their time. Yet wage theft – the systematic undercounting of overtime work – has shot through the roof. More often than not, the company you work for is not the company you seem to be working for. We like to think people are taking individual responsibility. But companies are shedding obligations to as much of their workforce as they can. Their goal is to lift revenue per employee. The more people they move off the balance sheet, the steeper that yield. During past recessions, productivity typically fell as companies cut back the volume of work they required their employees to do. The alternative would have been to embark on a painful round of layoffs. Now they need only cut back the supply of temps, which is painless and invisible. That is why corporate productivity held up during the Great Recession. The risk had been shifted onto the individual.

The numbers speak loudly enough. But they do not capture

the indignity people feel. Is the desire for respect an economic or a social aspiration? Or is it cultural? I would suggest the craving for dignity is universal. When people lose trust that society is treating them fairly, they drift into a deeper culture of mistrust. It should be little surprise that they come to view what the winners tell them with a toxic suspicion. Remind yourselves of how people reacted when the big banks were bailed out during the Great Recession. It was the taxpayer who picked up the bill. Ordinary people were still held to account. Millions of homes were repossessed. It is not enough to say that everyone would have been worse off if the banks had been allowed to go bankrupt. That was true. But society is not a balance sheet. People interpret the world in moral terms. They have narratives. The public noticed that the Obama administration failed to push through a single criminal conviction for what was the grandest rip-off in US financial history. Under Trump, we must get reacquainted with hearing about the world in Old Testament terms, yet I have no doubt Wall Street will still be deemed worthy of New Testament forgiveness.

Shortly after the election I got into a long talk with Karim Sajadpour, an American Muslim whose parents left Iran in the 1970s. Ordinarily, I would consult Karim about Iran and the Middle East – he is a specialist at a leading Washington think-tank. But few people, including Karim, could for any length of time keep their focus on work. Around the same time, Francis Fukuyama told me he had abandoned his research projects.

'Everything I've been working on for the past year suddenly feels trivial,' he said. 'The only topic I can think about is the future of liberal democracy.'[8] Karim felt the same way. Even though Trump's victory had put the Iran nuclear deal into question, Karim could not tear himself away from what was happening to America. Specifically, he was riveted to his home town of Midland, in Michigan. His parents had moved to Midland so his father could practise neurology. They still live there. Karim and his three siblings grew up there during the Iranian revolution and the American hostage crisis. It was a time of gas shortages. Images of angry Islamists burning American flags filled people's screens. The US diplomats were held for 444 days. As one of the very few Muslim families in a mostly blue-collar town, Karim says he would have been a natural target for people's angst. To heighten the Sajadpours' visibility, Karim's veil-wearing grand-mother lived with them. Yet he cannot recall one incident of racist abuse. 'Our background was occasionally a source of mild curiosity,' he said. 'But we were mostly noticed because of our athletic abilities . . . my brothers and I were very good at soccer.' Their closest friends were the Tessins, a Catholic family. Since Karim's dad earned a good living, they could afford to pay for help. 'In retrospect, what is notable was the fact that the folks who worked for my family – the nannies and cleaning ladies – were all locals,' says Karim. 'But we never noticed any resent-ment.' Neither do his parents today.

On 9 November, Karim was shocked to see his hometown

had voted overwhelmingly for Trump. He knew they were the same people with whom he had grown up. But he did not buy the view that they had suddenly turned into white nationalists. 'Like Trump voters everywhere, I am sure their reasons were complicated – but I don't find racism to be a compelling explanation,' he said. 'Putting an Iranian family in Midland at a time when Iranians are chanting "Death to America" would test any community's tolerance. Midland passed with flying colours.' Perhaps the people of Midland, which has suffered economically along with other parts of the Midwest, disliked being seen as deplorable. Maybe they wanted to take back control of their lives, however vaguely they had thought that through. Would that entail targeting Muslims, or expelling Mexicans? From Karim's story – and many others – it is hard to believe that was their ultimate motive. Yet it could become so. There is little doubt that is how Trump is interpreting his mandate. Democracy cannot survive for long in a swamp of mutual dislike. Depending on the society, most of the West is moving either towards populism or plutocracy. In some cases, such as the US, it is falling into a kind of hybrid pluto-populism that looks increasingly Latin American. Donald Trump's plans to deregulate Wall Street are a perfect illustration. Having railed against its greed on the campaign trail, he is now loosening the restraints on it in office. In the meantime, he plans to satisfy the populist urge by demonising illegal immigrants and Muslims, and indulging in theatre politics. Trump will operate as a kind of Ku Klux Kardashian, combining hard-right pugilism with the best of postmodern vaudeville. It is as though the French Bourbons have come back to life as twenty-first-century neo-liberals. They never learn. No matter what the challenge, cake and cheap diversion is the answer. Trump was supposed to have led a revolt against the elites. In practice, he wasted little time in laying out a tax-cutting and deregulatory banquet for their delectation. In marketing they call this bait and switch. The net effect of Trump's actual – as opposed to his rhetorical – economic agenda will be to deepen the economic conditions that gave rise to his candidacy.

It is not my aim to set out a detailed policy manifesto. Every grand remedy has its downsides. Setting up a Universal Basic Income – one solution that has attracted growing support – has broad meretricious appeal. Every citizen would receive a basic income of say £15,000 a year. All other welfare benefits would be scrapped, which would fund the whole thing. A UBI would cushion the losers in bad times and give them a springboard during the good. At a stroke it would also get rid of the vast bureaucratic apparatus that decides who qualifies for benefits and who doesn't. Goodbye to a million daily humiliations. But the UBI model has a couple of big flaws. First, it would create a powerful new magnet attracting immigrants to the Western world. Stopping them from arriving, and screening out those who slip through from claiming the basic income, would require even more draconian security. Second, a UBI would sever the link between effort and reward. People like to feel valued. Work is not just about economic reward. It is also about purpose and self-respect. Idleness is a soul-destroyer. Depression, divorce, despair and suicide all soar after six months of not working. Champions of UBI depict it as a magic wand for the complex problems we face. I fear it would help bring about a kind of Hunger Games, in which the poor are kept afloat while sating themselves on dog-eat-dog reality entertainment. UBI is also silent on the future of work.

We must think more radically than that. We must also bear in mind that anything we do will have global spillover effects. The developing world is making most of the capital goods that are used to displace the jobs of the middle-income people in the developed world. Their work is now increasingly devoted to looking after the rich.[9] Should we still cling to the idea that sending everybody to university is a solution? Apart from the fact that the impact of education reform would take twenty or more years to be felt, the machine is almost certainly moving faster. Technology would have long since overtaken updates to the curriculum. China and India are likely to have moved faster too. One critical goal must therefore be to lift the rewards of technical and service jobs in the West. In different areas, Germany, Scandinavia and other parts of Europe are good at this. By giving people genuine vocational skills, they raise the quality of what they do. The English-speaking world has forgotten how to do this. Instead of valuing high-quality service, society demands it at the lowest price. Another goal is to educate people to cope with a world in which machines are taking most of the old jobs. This means reviving a focus on the humanities, including basic levels of political literacy. Education should not just be about getting a job. It must equip us to be full members of society.

What would a new social compact look like? Since our crisis is political, the solutions must stretch far beyond economics. My own views do not always fit into twentieth-century pigeonholes. But I believe that protecting society's weakest from arbitrary misfortune is the ultimate test of our civilisational worth. It seems blindingly obvious that universal healthcare ought to be a basic shield against the vicissitudes of an increasingly volatile labour market. Humane immigration laws should be enforced, and the link between public benefits and citizenship restored. Ours is an age of lawyers and accountants. Micro-regulation of the workplace ought to be replaced with broad guidelines; free speech, in whatever form it takes, must be upheld on campuses and in the media; the tax system should be ruthlessly simplified; governments must tax bad things, such as carbon, rather than good things, like jobs; companies should be taxed where they conduct their business. Governments must launch Marshall Plans to retrain their middle classes. The nature of representative democracy should be re-imagined. Above all, money's stranglehold on the legislative process has to be broken.

Most of these, I take to be self-evident – though incomplete.

But whatever your remedies to the crisis of liberal democracy, nothing much is likely to happen unless the West's elites understand the enormity of what they face. If only out of self-preservation, the rich need to emerge from their postmodern Versailles. At the moment they seem busier shoring up its fortifications. In 2009, the Obama administration proposed a modest taxation of carried interest that would have treated a small slice of capital earnings as income. This would have taken a tiny bite out of the incomes of the largest hedge-fund and private-equity tycoons. As Warren Buffet said, 'It is not fair that I am paying lower taxes than my secretary.' Wall Street rose up in opposition. 'My administration is the only thing standing between you and the pitchforks,' Obama told bankers in 2009. Soon afterwards he climbed down. Stephen Schwarzman, one of America's wealthiest individuals, had compared Obama's modest tax proposal to Nazi expropriation. 'It's a war,' said Schwarzman, who is worth $11 billion. 'It's like when Hitler invaded Poland in 1939.'[10] You read that correctly. Eight years later Schwarzman was silent when Trump announced his Muslim travel ban. But he was jubilant at the news Trump was planning to scrap Obama's Wall Street reform. He had just been invited to head Trump's advisory council on growth and jobs. America's business outlook was 'infinitely better' than it had been for years, said Schwarzman. I very much doubt the future of Western democracy crossed his mind. He did not say anything about it. Nor did his peers – or at least not publicly. They were busy lobbying for their coming tax windfall, which promises to be huge, as Trump would say.

Ancient thinkers always thought the rich posed a greater threat to the republic than the poor: they cling on far more tenaciously to what they have. 'No tyrant ever conquered a city because he was poor and hungry,' said Aristotle. If nothing else, history offers us a vast early warning system. Let us hope we are capable of paying it some attention. As winter follows autumn, it is not Trump that I fear most – though he is scary enough. It is whoever might follow him.

———

Shortly before 9/11, I moved to India to be the *Financial Times's* South Asia bureau chief. I spent almost five years in New Delhi. I probably learned more from that experience than any other stage of my life. Among many other things, India taught me how easy it was in theory for a poor country to grow and how difficult it can be in practice. Finally, seventy years after independence, India is today the fastest-growing large economy on earth. It will take a decade or two at least before India will be forced to search within itself for growth. Until then, it should mostly come of its own accord. In the years ahead, the world will come to rely as much on India as it has on China to fuel global demand. As China ages, India will still be young. Many of the great questions facing humanity will be answered largely in India, China and Africa – not in the West. For the first time in centuries, the

West must get used to that. It has to learn the arts of persuasion
and compromise. One such imponderable is our species' ability
to tackle global warming, a subject that is beyond the scope of
this book. The future of war may also be settled somewhere up
in the roof of the world to which humanity's centre of gravity is
gradually shifting. But the biggest question is the future of politics. Divided by the Himalayas, the world's two largest countries,
China and India, sit side by side – one an autocracy, the other
a democracy. One had its revolution in 1949, the other became
a free country in 1947. It is as good a laboratory experiment as
you get.

In its opening decades, few people gave Indian democracy
much chance of survival. With the brief interregnum of Indira
Gandhi's emergency in the 1970s, Indian democracy has now
reached three score and ten. Though Narendra Modi, its current
prime minister, harbours Bonapartist traits, it is hard to imagine
he would try to close down the system. It is still harder to see
how he would succeed. So ingrained is India's culture of noisy
dissent and sheer pluralism that I would rate democracy as now
safer in India than in parts of the West. Half of the European
Union only adopted democracy in the late 1980s, and parts of
it are already having second thoughts. Pointing to India's pleth-
ora of religions, cults and political ideologies, E. P. Thompson,
the British historian, once said, 'There is not a thought that
is being thought in the West or the East that is not active in
some Indian mind.' But the biggest thing India has going for

it is growth. Though the caste system evolved into the most crushing and multilayered form of social humiliation the world has seen, there is an upside to that: things can only improve. And for the most part they are. No matter how bad inequality becomes – and in India the gulf between storied urban wealth and village poverty is obscene – most people are getting better off. Moreover, most Indians expect they will continue to get better off. It is an optimistic place. The same is true of much of Asia. With the exception of the Philippines, which is the least successful economy in South-East Asia, the strongest hope for democracy may increasingly be moving to the East. China's political future poses the biggest headache. Though it has grown faster than India, and looks after its poor far better, the gap between the two is starting to narrow. The future of China's politics is far less certain. China is in danger of growing old before it gets rich. But it is an immensely sophisticated country that is far more versatile than is so often portrayed. Though the Arab world is richer than India and on a par with China, most of its economies are heading in the wrong direction, which is ominous for the region's politics, and alarming for the rest of the world. Unless something breaks, the Arab world looks destined to keep chasing paradise lost. We can only hope the impact of Western populism does not send it further in the wrong direction.

Can the West regain its optimism? If the answer is no – and most of the portents are skewing the wrong way – liberal democracy will follow. If the next few years resemble the last, it is questionable whether Western democracy can take the strain. People have lost faith that their systems can deliver. More and more are looking backwards to a golden age that can never be regained. When a culture stops looking to the future, it loses a vital force. The search for Eden always ends in tears. The German author Thomas Mann once accused his peers of cultivating a 'sympathy for the abyss'. Cultural pessimism is rarely a helpful state of mind. Where one stands is inherently subjective. One person's Gomorrah might be another's hundred flowers in bloom. There is no precise measure of the health of liberal democracy. But we can be sure that America will not become great again under Trump. There will be a lethal mood of betrayal and frustration when he fails. Who knows where that could lead. It is comforting to assume, as many do, that the US system will simply revert to pre-Trump mode. The chances are at least as great that Trump will be able to pin the blame on elites, foreigners, Islam, minorities, unelected judges and other handy saboteurs. That is how populists operate. There is no rule that says populists fizzle out. As president, the means at Trump's disposal to divert public anger and target his enemies are chilling. At best, history is ambivalent on this question. Trump is no *deus ex machina*. The conditions that enabled his rise are only likely to deteriorate during his time in office. We should also fear whatever may follow Trump. Imagine how things would look with a competent and sophisticated white nationalist in the White House. In the years ahead, we must be especially alert to Benjamin Franklin's wise words: 'The price of liberty is eternal vigilance'. Liberal elites, in particular, will have to resist the temptation to carry on with their comfortable lives and imagine they are doing their part by signing up to the occasional Facebook protest. For Trump, if you are not against him you might as well be with him. Trump's opponents must also learn to separate the man from the people who vote for him. It would be lethal malpractice to continue writing off half of society as hidebound. Someone once said that the difference between erotica and pornography is the lighting. There is an equally hazy line between illiberal democracy and autocracy. We will know the difference when we see it.

NOTES

PREFACE

1 Francis Fukuyama, 'The End of History?', *National Interest* (summer 1989).
2 Eric Hobsbawm, *The Age of Extremes, 1941–1991* (Abacus, London, 1995).
3 Dan Jones, *Magna Carta: The Birth of Liberty* (Viking, New York, 2015), p. 4.
4 Interview with the author, January 2017.
5 Fareed Zakaria, *The Post-American World: And the Rise of the Rest* (Penguin, New York, 2009).
6 Henry Kissinger, *World Order* (Penguin, New York, 2014).

PART ONE: FUSION

1 Alexis de Tocqueville, *Democracy in America*, Part II (1840).
2 J. A. Hobson, *Imperialism: A Study* (James Pott & Company, New York, 1902), p. 333.
3 Jamil Anderlini and Lucy Hornby, 'China overtakes US as world's largest goods trader', *Financial Times*, 10 January 2014, <https://www.ft.com/content/7c2dbd70-79a6-11e3-b381-00144feabdco>.
4 Branko Milanovic, *Global Inequality: A New Approach for the Age of Globalization* (Belknap Press, Cambridge MA, 2016 (ebook)).

5 Danny Quah, 'The Global Economy's Shifting Centre of Gravity', *Global Policy*, 2:1 (January 2011), <http://onlinelibrary.wiley.com/doi/10.1111/j.1758-5899.2010.00066.x/pdf>.

6 Milanovic, *Global Inequality*.

7 Hobson, *Imperialism*, p. 339.

8 Milanovic, *Global Inequality*.

9 Richard Baldwin: *The Great Convergence: Information Technology and the New Globalization* (Belknap Press, Cambridge MA, 2016 (ebook)).

10 Hugh White, *The China Choice: Why We Should Share Power* (Oxford University Press, Oxford, 2012 (ebook)).

11 The World Economic Forum's website has a comprehensive database of each forum's reports and sessions stretching back many years. For 2016, see: <https://www.weforum.org/events/world-economic-forum-annual-meeting-2016/sessions/the-global-economic-outlook-1d2286ef-25a9-47cf-bba6-56fc8ef98004>.

12 Chris Giles, 'China poised to pass US as world's leading economic power this year', *Financial Times*, 30 April 2014, <https://www.ft.com/content/d79ffff8-cfb7-11e3-9b2b-00144feabdc0>.

13 John Williamson, 'From reform agenda to damaged brand name: A short history of the Washington Consensus and suggestions for what to do next', *Finance and Development*, 40:3 (September 2003). Available at <https://people.ucsc.edu/~hutch/Econ143/historywash.pdf>.

14 Robert H. Frank, *Success and Luck: Good Fortune and the Myth of Meritocracy* (Princeton University Press, Princeton, 2016), p. 71.

15 Milanovic, *Global Inequality*. Milanovic's book is seminal; I would urge anyone interested in the future of globalisation to read it. I have borrowed liberally from his statistics.

16 Ibid.

17 Frank, *Success and Luck*, p. 114.

18 These figures are cited frequently in public by Lawrence H. Summers.

19 *Financial Times*, 20 June 2016, <https://www.ft.com/content/a5d5a8fe-36f5-11e6-a780-b48ed7b6126f>, and Edward Luce,

'US workforce dropouts explain Donald Trump's rise', *Financial Times*, 21 June 2016, <https://www.ft.com/content/5c8d0758-37c4-11e6-9a05-82a9b15a8ee7>.

20 Edward Luce, 'Drugs, painkillers and the New Hampshire primary', *Financial Times*, 7 February 2016, <https://www.ft.com/content/78d5ba76-cbff-11e5-a8ef-ea66e967dd44>.

21 Anne Case and Angus Deaton, 'Rising Morbidity and Mortality in Midlife among White Non-Hispanic Americans in the 21st Century', *Proceedings of the National Academy of Sciences of the United States of America*, 112:49 (2015), <http://www.pnas.org/content/112/49/15078.full>.

22 Benjamin M. Friedman, *The Moral Consequences of Economic Growth* (Vintage, New York, 2006 (ebook)).

23 Adam Smith, *The Wealth of Nations*, Book 1 (1776).

24 Central Intelligence Agency, *The World Fact Book 2016* (Central Intelligence Agency, Washington DC, 2016), <https://www.cia.gov/library/publications/the-world-factbook/fields/2177.html>.

25 Tyler Cowen, *The Complacent Class: The Self-Defeating Quest for the American Dream* (St Martin's Press, New York, 2017), p. 82.

26 Ibid., p. 12.

27 Milanovic, *Global Inequality*.

28 Stephen S. Cohen and J. Bradford DeLong, *Concrete Economics: The Hamilton Approach to Economic Growth and Policy* (Harvard Business Review Press, Boston, 2016), p. 10.

29 Milanovic, *Global Inequality*.

30 Frank, *Success and Luck*, p. 51.

31 Raj Chetty, David Grusky, Maximilian Hell, Nathaniel Hedren, Robert Manduca and Jimmy Narang, 'The fading American dream: trends in absolute income mobility since 1940', National Bureau for Economic Research working paper No. 22910 (December 2016), <http://www.nber.org/papers/w22910>.

32 Frank, *Success and Luck*, p. 8.

33 Richard Reeves, *Dream Hoarders: How the American Upper Middle Class Is Leaving Everyone Else in the Dust, Why That Is a*

Problem, and What to Do about It (Brookings Institution Press, Washington DC, 2016).

34 'Some colleges have more students from the top 1 per cent than the bottom 60 per cent', *New York Times*, 17 January 2017, <https://www.nytimes.com/interactive/2017/01/18/upshot/some-colleges-have-more-students-from-the-top-1-percent-than-the-bottom-60.html?_r=0>.

35 Frank Newport, 'Fewer Americans identify as middle class', Gallup, 28 April 2015, <http://www.gallup.com/poll/182918/fewer-americans-identify-middle-class-recent-years.aspx>.

36 Michael Young, 'Down with meritocracy', *Guardian*, 28 June 2001, <https://www.theguardian.com/politics/2001/jun/29/comment>.

37 I elaborate this point in my column 'The end of American meritocracy', *Financial Times*, 8 May 2016, <https://www.ft.com/content/c17d402a-12cf-11e6-839f-2922947098f0>.

38 Joe Coscarelli, 'Spike Lee's amazing rant against gentrification: "We been here!"', *New York Magazine*, 25 February 2014, <http://nymag.com/daily/intelligencer/2014/02/spike-lee-amazing-rant-against-gentrification.html>.

39 Richard Florida, *The New Urban Crisis: How Our Cities Are Increasing Inequality, Deepening Segregation, and Failing the Middle Class – and What We Can Do About It* (Basic Books, New York, 2017), p. 132.

40 Ibid.

41 Ibid., p. 191.

42 Ibid., p. 159.

43 Mark Muro and Sifan Liu, 'Another Clinton-Trump divide: high-output America versus low-output America', Brookings, 29 November 2016, <https://www.brookings.edu/blog/the-avenue/2016/11/29/another-clinton-trump-divide-high-output-america-vs-low-output-america/>.

44 I draw this insightful point from Richard C. Longworth's cogent 'On Global Cities', Chicago Council on Global Affairs, 21 May 2005, <https://www.thechicagocouncil.org/publication/global-cities>.

45 Findings are throughout Richard Florida's *The New Urban Crisis*.

46 Melkorka Licea, '"Poor door" tenants of luxury tower reveal the financial apartheid within', *New York Post*, 17 January 2016, <http://nypost.com/2016/01/17/poor-door-tenants-reveal-luxury-towers-financial-apartheid/>.

47 Milanovic, *Global Inequality*.

48 Florida, *The New Urban Crisis*, p. 41.

49 Ibid, p. 38.

50 Cowen, *The Complacent Class*, p. 7.

51 Florida, *The New Urban Crisis*, p. 216.

52 Martin Ford, *Rise of the Robots: Technology and the Threat of a Jobless Future* (Basic Books, New York, 2015 (ebook)).

53 Ibid.

54 Ibid.

55 Lawrence Mishel, 'Entry-level workers' wages fell in lost decade', Economic Policy Institute report, 7 March 2012, <http://www.epi.org/publication/ib327-young-workers-wages/>.

56 Baldwin, *The Great Convergence*.

57 William J. Bernstein, *The Birth of Plenty: How the Prosperity of the Modern World was Created* (McGraw-Hill, New York, 2004).

58 *Occupational Outlook Handbook*, Bureau of Labor Statistics, <https://www.bls.gov/ooh/>.

59 Robert J. Gordon, *The Rise and Fall of American Growth: The US Standard of Living since the Civil War* (Princeton University Press, Princeton, 2016), p. ix.

60 Ibid. p. 3.

61 Ibid., p. 4.

62 For my own treatment of Gordon and Cohen and DeLong's books, see 'Is robust American growth a thing of the past?', *Financial Times*, 19 February 2016, <https://www.ft.com/content/80c3164e-d644-11e5-8887-98e7feb46f27>.

63 Gordon, *The Rise and Fall of American Growth*, p. 13.

64 James Manyika, Susan Lund, Jacques Bughin, Kelsey Robinson, Jan Mischke and Deepa Mahajan, 'Independent Work: Choice, necessity and the gig economy', McKinsey Global

Institute report, October 2016, <http://www.mckinsey.com/global-themes/employment-and-growth/independent-work-choice-necessity-and-the-gig-economy>.

65 Ibid.

66 Ibid.

67 Ibid.

68 Jaron Lanier, *Who Owns the Future?* (Simon & Schuster, New York, 2013 (ebook)).

69 Edward Luce, 'Obama must face the rise of the robots', *Financial Times*, 3 February 2013, <https://www.ft.com/content/f6f19228-6bbc-11e2-a17d-00144feab49a>.

70 Lee Drutman and Yascha Mounk, 'When the Robots Rise', *National Interest*, 144 (July–August 2016), <http://nationalinterest.org/feature/when-the-robots-rise-16830>.

71 Espen Barth Eide, '2015: the year geopolitics bites back?', World Economic Forum, 7 November 2014, <https://www.weforum.org/agenda/2014/11/2015-year-geostrategic-competition/>.

72 Global Risks 2015, World Economic Forum, <https://reports.weforum.org/global-risks-2015/part-2-risks-in-focus/2-2-global-risks-arising-from-the-accelerated-interplay-between-geopolitics-and-economics/>.

73 Global Risks 2017, World Economic Forum, <http://reports.weforum.org/global-risks-2017/part-2-social-and-political-challenges/2-1-western-democracy-in-crisis/>.

74 Ibid.

75 Lawrence Summers, 'America needs to make a new case for trade', *Financial Times*, 27 April 2008, <http://www.ft.com/cms/s/0/c35d3d62-14ba-11dd-a741-0000779fd2ac.html?ft_site=falcon&desktop=true#axzz4YDkDxH19>.

76 Lawrence Summers, 'Voters deserve responsible nationalism not reflex globalism', *Financial Times*, 9 July 2016, <https://www.ft.com/content/15598db8-4456-11e6-9b66-0712b3873ae1>.

77 Dani Rodrik, *The Globalization Paradox: Democracy and the Future of the World Economy* (W. W. Norton & Company, New York, 2011).

78 Thomas L. Friedman, *The Lexus and the Olive Tree: Understanding Globalization* (Farrar, Straus & Giroux, New York, 2000).

PART TWO: REACTION

1 Samuel Huntington describes mid-1970s Europe onwards as the 'third wave', but my starting date is different.

2 Peter Pomerantsev, *Nothing Is True and Everything Is Possible: The Surreal Heart of the New Russia* (Basic Books, New York, 2014 (ebook)).

3 Alexander Cooley, 'Countering Democratic Norms', in Larry Diamond, Marc F. Plattner and Christopher Walker (eds), *Authoritarianism Goes Global: The Challenge to Democracy* (Johns Hopkins University Press, Baltimore, 2016).

4 Ibid.

5 *Freedom in the World 2016*, Freedom House, <https://freedomhouse.org/report/freedom-world/freedom-world-2016>.

6 Interview with the author, January 2017.

7 Andrew Nathan, 'China's Challenge', in Diamond, Plattner and Walker (eds), *Authoritarianism Goes Global.*

8 Geoff Dyer and George Parker, 'US attacks UK's "constant accommodation" with China', *Financial Times*, 12 March 2015, <https://www.ft.com/content/31c4880a-c8d2-11e4-bc64-00144feab7de>.

9 Cooley, 'Countering Democratic Norms'.

10 Ibid.

11 Eric X. Li, 'Watching American Democracy in China', *Foreign Affairs*, June 2016, <https://www.foreignaffairs.com/articles/china/2016-04-19/watching-american-democracy-china>.

12 Quoted as epigraph to Jan-Werner Müller, *What Is Populism?* (University of Pennsylvania Press, Philadelphia, 2016).

13 Edward Luce, 'Hillary Clinton's rickety bridge to the White House', *Financial Times*, 30 November 2014, <https://www.ft.com/content/e84aa190-76f2-11e4-8273-00144feabdc0>.

14 Peter Mair, *Ruling the Void: The Hollowing of Western Democracy* (Verso, New York, 2013 (ebook)).

15 Jeffrey M. Jones, 'In US, new record 43% are political inde-
    pendents', Gallup, 7 January 2015, <http://www.gallup.com/
    poll/180440/new-record-political-independents.aspx>.
16 Mair, *Ruling the Void*.
17 Robert Ford and Matthew Goodwin, *Revolt on the Right:
    Explaining Support for the Radical Right in Britain* (Routledge, New
    York, 2014 (ebook)).
18 Müller, *What Is Populism?*
19 Quoted in Ford and Goodwin, *Revolt on the Right*.
20 Edward Luce, 'Tony Blair warns US Democrats against support-
    ing Bernie Sanders', *Financial Times*, 23 February 2016, <https://
    www.ft.com/content/9c70cae8-da55-11e5-98fd-06d75973fe09>.
21 Julia Carrie Wong and Danny Yadron, 'Hillary Clinton pro-
    poses student debt deferral for startup founders', *Guardian*, 29
    June 2016, <https://www.theguardian.com/us-news/2016/jun/28/
    hillary-clinton-student-debt-proposal-startup-tech-founders>.
22 <https://www.hillaryclinton.com/issues/>.
23 William H. Frey, 'New projections point to a majority minor-
    ity nation in 2044', Brookings Institution, 12 December
    2014, <https://www.brookings.edu/blog/the-avenue/2014/12/12/
    new-projections-point-to-a-majority-minority-nation-in-2044/>.
24 The Hispanic population, 2010. US Census, <http://www.census.
    gov/prod/cen2010/briefs/c2010br-04.pdf>.
25 Harry Enten, 'Trump probably did better with Latino voters
    than Romney did', FiveThirtyEight, 18 November 2016, <https://
    fivethirtyeight.com/features/trump-probably-did-better-with-latino-
    voters-than-romney-did/>.
26 Amitai Etzioni, 'Adding census categories won't unite a
    divided America', *National Interest*, 8 January 2017, <http://
    nationalinterest.org/feature/adding-census-categories-wont-unite-
    divided-america-18984>.
27 Mark Lilla, 'The end of identity liberalism', *New York Times*, 18
    November 2016, <https://www.nytimes.com/2016/11/20/opinion/
    sunday/the-end-of-identity-liberalism.html>.
28 'Columbia professor says Democrats need to move beyond

identity politics', NPR, 25 November 2016, <http://www.npr.
org/2016/11/25/503316461/columbia-professor-says-democrats-need-
to-move-beyond-identity-politics>.

29 Lilla, 'The end of identity liberalism'.

30 At the 2013 UKIP annual conference. See Sean Clare,
    'Nigel Farage: Britain would prosper outside EU', BBC News,
    20 September 2013, <http://www.bbc.com/news/uk-politics-
    24163335>.

31 Ford and Goodwin, *Revolt on the Right.*

32 Ibid.

33 *Social Insurance in Sweden*, Government Offices of Sweden hand-
    book on benefits, <http://www.government.se/49b756/contentassets/
    48c6a2996f844d54bd2ad77dbc56bac9/social-insurance-in-sweden-
    s2014.010>.

34 Interview with the author, January 2017.

35 Takis S. Pappas, 'Distinguishing Liberal Democracy's Challengers',
    Journal of Democracy, 27:4 (October 2016), p. 27.

36 Ibid., p. 30.

37 Alec Tyson and Shiva Maniam, 'Behind Trump's victory: Divisions
    by race, gender, education', Pew Research, 9 November 2016, <http://
    www.pewresearch.org/fact-tank/2016/11/09/behind-trumps-
    victory-divisions-by-race-gender-education/>.

38 Didier Eribon (trans. Michael Lucey), *Returning to Reims*
    (Semiotext, New York, 2007).

39 J. D. Vance, *Hillbilly Elegy: A Memoir of a Family and Culture in
    Crisis* (Harper, New York, 2016).

40 Eribon, *Returning to Reims.*

41 Quoted in Müller, *What Is Populism?*

42 Tim Kreider, 'I love America. It's Americans I hate', *The
    Week*, 9 January 2017, <http://theweek.com/articles/670637/
    love-america-americans-hate>.

43 Roger Scruton, *A Political Philosophy* (A. & C. Black, London,
    2006), p. 25.

44 Quoted in Nancy Isenberg, *White Trash: The 400-Year Untold
    History of Class in America* (Viking, New York, 2016).

45 Quoted in Bernard Crick, *Democracy: A Very Short Introduction* (Oxford University Press, Oxford, 2002).

46 Sean Wilentz, *Andrew Jackson: The American Presidents Series: The 7th President 1829–1837* (Times Books, New York, 2007).

47 Ibid., p. 70.

48 Quoted in Crick, *Democracy*.

49 Müller, *What Is Populism?*

50 For an excellent treatment of this read *Democracy for Realists: Why Elections Do Not Produce Responsive Government* by Christopher H. Achen and Larry Bartels (Princeton University Press, Princeton, 2016).

51 Cas Mudde, 'The problem with populism', *Guardian*, 17 February 2015, <https://www.theguardian.com/commentisfree/2015/feb/17/problem-populism-syriza-podemos-dark-side-europe>.

52 The WVS findings are brilliantly dissected in Roberto Stefan Foa and Yascha Mounk, 'The Danger of Deconsolidation', *Journal of Democracy*, 27:3 (July 2016), <http://www.journalofdemocracy.org/sites/default/files/Foa%26Mounk-27-3.pdf>.

53 Ibid.

54 I thank Foa and Mounk for this thought-provoking inversion.

55 Matt Rocheleau, 'Trump's Cabinet picks so far worth a combined $13b', *Boston Globe*, 20 December 2016, <https://www.bostonglobe.com/metro/2016/12/20/trump-cabinet-picks-far-are-worth-combined/XvAJmHCgkHhO3lSxgIKvRM/story.html>.

56 Chris Hedges, *Empire of Illusion: The End of Literacy and the Triumph of Spectacle* (Nation Books, New York, 2009).

57 Alexis de Tocqueville, *Democracy in America*, Part I (1835).

58 Nicholas Negroponte, *Being Digital* (Hodder & Stoughton, London, 1996).

59 Quoted in Evgeny Morozov, *The Net Delusion: The Dark Side of Internet Freedom* (Basic Books, New York, 2012).

60 Henry David Thoreau, *Walden* (1854; W. W. Norton, New York, 1966), p. 67.

61 Morozov, *The Net Delusion*. Morozov's book is a compelling read for anyone interested in technology and democracy.

62 'The Revolution Will Be Twittered', *Atlantic*, 13 June 2009, <https://www.theatlantic.com/daily-dish/archive/2009/06/the-revolution-will-be-twittered/200478/>.

63 From Pomerantsev, *Nothing Is True and Everything Is Possible*.

64 Michael M. Grynbaum, 'Trump strategist Stephen Bannon says media should "Keep its mouth shut"', *New York Times*, 26 January 2017, <https://www.nytimes.com/2017/01/26/business/media/stephen-bannon-trump-news-media.html?_r=0>.

65 Paul Vitello, 'Randolph Thrower, IRS chief who resisted Nixon, dies at 100', *New York Times*, 18 March 2014, <https://www.nytimes.com/2014/03/19/us/randolph-w-thrower-dies-at-100-ran-irs-under-nixon.html>.

66 Quoted in George Lardner Jr, 'Nixon sought "ruthless" chief to "do what he's told" at IRS', *Washington Post*, 3 January 1997, <https://www.washingtonpost.com/archive/politics/1997/01/03/nixon-sought-ruthless-chief-to-do-what-hes-told-at-irs/6a9dbd0a-0261-4afe-9402-21b154bb20bd/?utm_term=.de0816f4e7e3>.

67 Douglas Martin, 'Johnnie M. Walters, IRS chief who resisted Nixon's pressure, dies at 94', *New York Times*, 26 June 2014, <https://www.nytimes.com/2014/06/26/us/politics/johnnie-m-walters-ex-irs-chief-dies-at-94.html>.

68 I am indebted to Mike Lofgren for his excellent book *The Deep State: The Fall of the Constitution and the Rise of a Shadow Government* (Penguin, New York, 2016).

69 The story is recounted well by Ezra Klein in 'The snake', *Vox*, 30 January 2017, <http://www.vox.com/policy-and-politics/2017/1/30/14427228/donald-trump-snake-story-refugees>.

70 Salena Zito, 'Taking Trump seriously, not literally', *Atlantic*, 23 September 2016, <https://www.theatlantic.com/politics/archive/2016/09/trump-makes-his-case-in-pittsburgh/501335/>.

71 Crick, *Democracy*.

PART THREE: FALLOUT

1 Jake Sherman, 'Poll: voters liked Trump's "America First" address', *Politico*, 25 January 2017, <http://www.politico.com/story/2017/01/poll-voters-liked-trumps-inaugural-address-234148>.

2 Dana Priest, 'The disruptive career of Michael Flynn, Trump's national-security adviser', *New Yorker*, 23 November 2016, <http://www.newyorker.com/news/news-desk/the-disruptive-career-of-trumps-national-security-adviser>.

3 J. Lester Feder, 'This is how Stephen Bannon sees the entire world', Buzzfeed, 16 November 2016. Transcript of a 2014 speech by Bannon via Skype to a conference in the Vatican in 2014: <https://www.buzzfeed.com/lesterfeder/this-is-how-steve-bannon-sees-the-entire-world>.

4 I am indebted to Jonathan David Kirshner, of Cornell University, whose paper 'Keynes's Early Beliefs and Why They Still Matter' (*Challenge*, 58:5 (October 2015)) brilliantly elucidates the evolution in Keynes's thinking.

5 Graham Allison, 'The Thucydides Trap: Are the US and China Headed for War?', *Atlantic*, 24 September 2015, <https://www.theatlantic.com/international/archive/2015/09/united-states-china-war-thucydides-trap/406756/>.

6 David Calleo, 'Introduction: Decline: American Style', in Benjamin M. Rowland (ed.), *Is The West in Decline?: Historical, Military, and Economic Perspectives* (Lexington Books, Lanham, 2016).

7 Hugh White, *The China Choice: Why We Should Share Power* (Oxford University Press, Oxford, 2012).

8 Jagdish Bhagwati, 'A New Vocabulary for Trade', YaleGlobal Online, 4 August 2005, <http://yaleglobal.yale.edu/content/new-vocabulary-trade>.

9 For more on this consult Lanxin Xiang's essay, 'Decline and Rise of China: A New Perspective', in Rowland (ed.), *Is the West in Decline?*

10 Henry Kissinger, *World Order* (Penguin, New York, 2014).

11 Paul Krugman, 'The myth of Asia's miracle', *Foreign Affairs*, 73:6 (November/December 1994), <http://econ.sciences-po.fr/sites/default/files/file/myth_of_asias-miracle.pdf>.

12 Kishore Mahbubani, *The Great Convergence: Asia, the West, and the Logic of One World* (Public Affairs, New York, 2013). Perhaps the most cogent book on Asia's ambivalence on US leadership.

13 In an email correspondence with the author.

14 Kissinger, *World Order*.

15 This is not to downplay Roosevelt's shameful wartime internment of Japanese-Americans, nor Britain's decision to round up all German nationals, including German-Jewish refugees.

16 Kissinger, *World Order*. Kissinger summarises the analogy well.

17 It is worth reading Obama's speech in full: <http://www.ploughshares.org/sites/default/files/newss/Palm%20Sunday%20Speech.pdf?_ga=1.140094451.152788391.1486684037>.

18 Again, worth watching Trump talking about nuclear weapons. Interview with Chris Matthews, MSNBC: <https://www.youtube.com/watch?v=Gpxr9ZUp7No>.

19 Robert MacMillan, 'The warhead at the top of the pack: The Reuters/Donald Trump interview', Reuters, 24 February 2017, <http://www.reuters.com/article/us-select-24feb-idUSKBN1631Uo>.

20 This anecdote gave Kaplan the title for his book.

21 Shawn Donnan, 'US trade chief seeks to reshore supply chain', *Financial Times*, 31 January 2017, <https://www.ft.com/content/8dc63502-e7c7-11e6-893c-082c54a7f539>.

22 Cited in Branko Milanovic, *Global Inequality: A New Approach for the Age of Globalization* (Belknap Press, Cambridge MA, 2016).

23 Andrew E. Kramer, 'The phrase Putin never uses about terrorism (and Trump does)', *New York Times*, 1 February 2017, <https://www.nytimes.com/2017/02/01/world/europe/vladimir-putin-donald-trump-terrorism.html>.

Part Four: Half Life

1 Becky Bowers, 'President Barack Obama's shifting stance on gay marriage', *Politifact*, 11 May 2012, <http://www.politifact.com/truth-o-meter/statements/2012/may/11/barack-obama/president-barack-obamas-shift-gay-marriage/>.

2 Edward Luce, 'Why Cleveland will be haunted by the ghosts of Chicago', *Financial Times*, 10 April 2016, <https://www.ft.com/content/f2239c18-ff08-11e5-99cb-83242733f755>.

3 Edward Luce, 'The end of American meritocracy', *Financial Times*, 8 May 2016, <https://www.ft.com/content/c17d402a-12cf-11e6-839f-2922947098f0>.

4 'Transcript: "This is your victory," says Obama', CNN. Transcript of Obama's 2008 Chicago victory speech: <http://edition.cnn.com/2008/POLITICS/11/04/obama.transcript/>.

5 Tamara Draut, *Sleeping Giant: How the New Working Class Will Transform America* (Doubleday, New York, 2016), p. 3.

6 Ibid., p. 58.

7 Ibid., p. 2.

8 Interview with the author, January 2017. A note about Fukuyama: Though I have criticised his End of History thesis, as has become habitual among many people, I consider him to be one of the most subtle, knowledgeable and reflective thinkers alive today. He is also true to Keynes's dictum, 'When the facts change, I change my mind. What do you do, sir?' If Fukuyama hadn't written it, we would have had to invent it.

9 My paraphrasing of Branko Milanovic's description of the global division of labour.

10 Courtney Comstock, 'Steve Schwarzman on tax increases: "It's like when Hitler invaded Poland"', *Business Insider*, 16 August 2010, <http://www.businessinsider.com/steve-schwarzman-taxes-hitler-invaded-poland-2010-8?IR=T>.

ACKNOWLEDGEMENTS

I have written ambitious books on large topics before. But nothing compares to a slim volume on the future of Western liberal democracy. It seems preposterous that a single author would dare address such a deep, wide-ranging and historically complex subject spanning such a diverse range of countries – and in such short order. I make no apologies for trying. We are cursed today by increasingly narrow academic specialisation. By definition, there can be no such thing as an expert in such a multi-disciplinary endeavour. As a citizen of one democratic country, a resident of another, a former resident of four other democratic countries, and a frequent traveller to many more, I feel a passion about our political future that is inevitably greater than the depth of my knowledge. I am also father to a young daughter, Mimi. When I think of her future, it is increasingly with fear as well as hope. Everyone is qualified to worry about the society their children will grow up in. When I think of my now-octogenarian parents, it is with an added sense of poignancy. I know they worry as much as they have at any time in their lives about the future of our world. The next generation down may be powerless to change some things. But we are surely capable of preventing our societies' slide into a new dark age.

My first thanks go to my wonderfully generous and wise agent, Natasha Fairweather, who came up with the idea of a book on this subject shortly after Donald Trump's victory. Without Natasha's encouragement I would never have dreamt of taking it on. As she pointed out, I could spend the rest of my life researching a multi-volume disquisition on the subject and die with it uncompleted. There is no time like the present – particularly *this* present. Equally, I would like to underline my deep thanks to Morgan Entrekin of Grove Atlantic and Tim Whiting of Little, Brown, who both so enthusiastically and instinctively took on this book project. Without their vote of confidence – and their expert guidance – this book would not have been written. I have also been very fortunate to have two highly accomplished and eagle-eyed editors – Zoe Gullen in London and Allison Malecha in New York. My gratitude for their felicity with detail as well as their professional alacrity. A number of people read speedily through the manuscript and provided excellent feedback. Any errors of judgement that remain are my own. But each was generous with their time and insights. My deepest thanks go to Ivo Daalder, Pratap Bhanu Mehta,

Mat Burrows, Krishna Guha, Niamh King, Rachel Bronson and Luigi Zingales. I have also benefited greatly from the insights of Michael Lind of the New America Foundation, whose work on the trajectory of US democracy and whose conversations with me on and around many of the topics addressed in this book have proved invaluable. Michael deserves far greater recognition for anticipating the crisis we find ourselves confronting. Others who have kindly lent me their brains on a frequent basis, and to whom I am deeply grateful, include Tyler Cowen, Jonathan Rauch, Larry Summers, David Rothkopf, Martin Wolf, Jonathan Kirshner, Bill Galston, E. J. Dionne, Thomas Wright, Richard Porter, Eric Li, Lloyd Green, Alexander Dynkin, Steve Clemons, David Frum, John Pethkoukis, Jane Mayer, Tom Friedman, Matthias Matthjis, William Wallis, Sidney Blumenthal, Karim Sajadpour, Yascha Mounk, Francis Fukuyama, Niall Ferguson, Lou Susman, Richard Longworth, Kori Schake and Liaquat Ahamed. My apologies to the many people whom I have left out. I would also like to thank the *Financial Times* for giving me the opportunity to write as a columnist and general writer. It is a huge privilege to be employed by the pre-eminent global newspaper and to work among such collegiate and talented journalists. My profound thanks to the *FT* for giving me the time and space at very short notice to write this book.

Finally, I would like to thank the two most important people in my life. My daughter, Mimi, who gives me joy and perspective. I have caught her more than once selling spare copies of my last book on our doorstep during her periodic summer lemonade sales. I only ask that she make a slightly less generous discount for this one. I would like to dedicate this book to Niamh King, my partner, who is my best friend as well as my love. Without Niamh nothing would make sense. If everyone were even a tiny bit like Niamh, there would be no need for a book like this. Liberal democracy would be safe. I cannot imagine having written this book without her.

INDEX

advertising, 65–6, 178
Afghanistan, 80
Africa: Chinese investment in, 32,
    84; economic growth in, 21, 31,
    32; future importance of, 200–1;
    and liberal democracy, 82, 83, 183;
    migration from, 140, 181; slave
    trade, 23, 55, 56
African-Americans, 104
age demographics, 34–5, 155, 156;
    ageing populations, 39; baby boom
    years, 39, 121; and gig economy,
    64; life expectancy, 38, 58, 59,
    60; millennials, 40–1, 121–2; and
    support for democracy, 121–2; and
    voter turnout, 103–4
Airbnb, 63
Albright, Madeleine, 6
American Revolution, 9
Andorra, 72
Andreessen, Marc, 61
Apple, 27, 31, 59, 60, 156
Arab Spring, 12, 82
Arab world, 202
Arendt, Hannah, *The Origins of
    Totalitarianism*, 128
Aristotle, 138, 200
artificial intelligence, 13, 34, 51–5, 56,
    60–2
Asian Development Bank, 84
Asian economies, 21–2, 162; as engine
    of global growth, 21, 30, 31, 32; and

Industrial Revolution, 23–4; and
    optimism, 202; of South Asia, 31;
    see also China; India
Asian flu crisis (1997), 29
Asian Infrastructure Investment Bank
    (AIIB), 84
Attlee, Clement, 90
Australia, 84, 160, 167, 175
Austria, 15–16, 116
autocracy: and America's post-9/11
    blunders, 80–1, 85, 86;
    authoritarian nature of Trump, 133,
    169, 171, 178–9; China as, 78, 80,
    83–6, 159–60, 165, 201; and end of
    Cold War, 5, 78–9; and First World
    War, 115; and Great Recession,
    83–4; and illiberal democracy, 204;
    myth of as more efficient, 170–1;
    popular demagogues, 137; rising
    support for, 11, 73, 82–3, 122
automation: and Chinese workforce,
    62, 169; communications
    technology, 13, 52–5, 56–7,
    59–60, 61–6, 67–8 *see also* digital
    revolution; and education, 197,
    198; and Henry Ford, 66–7;
    political responses to, 67–8;
    steam revolution, 24, 55–6;
    techno-optimists, 52, 60; in
    transport, 54, 55, 56–7, 58, 59, 61

Bagehot, Walter, 115

Baker Institute, 68
Baldwin, Richard, 25, 27, 61
Bangladesh, 32
bank bail-outs, 193
Bannon, Steve, 130, 148, 173, 181–2
Belgium, 140
Bell, Daniel, 37
Berlin Wall, fall of (1989), 3–5, 6, 7,
   74, 77
Bernstein, Carl, 132
Berra, Yogi, 57
Bhagwati, Jagdish, 159
Bismarck, Otto von, 42, 78, 120, 156,
   161
Black Death, 25
Blair, Tony, 45, 89–90, 91
Blum, Léon, 116
Boer War (1899-1902), 155, 156
Bortnikov, Alexander, 6
Botswana, 82
Brazil, 29
Brecht, Bertolt, 86, 87
Breitbart News, 148
Brexit, 15, 73, 88, 92, 98, 101, 104, 119,
   120, 163; UKIP's NHS spending
   claim, 102; urban–hinterland split
   in vote, 47, 48, 130; xenophobia
   during campaign, 100–1
Britain: elite responses to Nazi
   Germany, 117; foreign policy goals,
   179; gig economy, 63; growth of
   inequality in modern era, 43, 46,
   47, 48, 50–1; history in popular
   imagination, 163; Imperial
   Preference, 22; London's elites,
   98–100, 130; nineteenth-century
   franchise extension, 114–15;
   policy towards China, 164; rapid
   expansion in nineteenth century,
   24; and rise of Germany, 156, 157;
   rising support for authoritarianism,
   122; separatism within, 140;
   Thatcher's electoral success,
   189–90
British East India Company, 22
British National Party (BNP), 100
Brown, Gordon, 99
Brownian movement, 172

Bryan, William Jennings, 111
Brynjolfsson, Erik, 60
Buffet, Warren, 199
Bush, George W., 31, 73, 79–81, 103,
   156, 157, 163, 165, 182
Bush Republicans, 189

Cameron, David, 15, 92, 98, 99–100
Carnegie, Andrew, 42–3
Cherokee Indians, 114, 134
Chicago, 48
China: as autocracy, 78, 80, 83–6,
   159–60, 165, 201; circular view of
   history, 11; colonial exploitation
   of, 20, 22–3, 55; decoupling of
   economy from West (2008), 29–30,
   83–4; democracy activists in, 86,
   140; entry to WTO (2001), 26;
   exceptionalism, 166; expulsion
   of Western NGOs, 85; future
   importance of, 200–1; and global
   trading system, 19–20, 26–7; Great
   Firewall in, 129; handover of
   Hong Kong (1997), 163–4; history
   in popular imagination, 163–4;
   hostility to Western liberalism,
   84–6, 159–60, 162; and hydrogen
   bomb, 163; and Industrial
   Revolution, 22, 23–4; internal
   migration in, 41; investment in
   developing countries, 32, 84;
   military expansion, 157, 158;
   as nuclear power, 175; Obama's
   trip to (2009), 159–60; political
   future of, 168–9, 202; pragmatic
   development route, 28, 29–30;
   pre-Industrial Revolution economy,
   22; rapid expansion of, 13, 20–2,
   25–8, 30, 35, 58, 157, 159; and
   robot economy, 62; Shanghai
   Cooperation Organization, 80;
   Trump's promised trade war, 135,
   145, 149; and Trump's victory,
   85–6, 140; US naval patrols in
   seas off, 148, 158, 165; US policy
   towards, 25–6, 145–6, 157–61, 165;
   US–China war scenario, 145–53,
   161; in Western thought, 161–2;

Xi's crackdown on internal dissent, 168; Zheng He's naval fleet, 165–6
China Central Television (CCTV), 84, 85
Christianity, 10, 105
Churchill, Winston, 98, 117, 128, 169
cities, 47–51, 130
class: creeping gentrification, 46, 48, 50–1; emerging middle classes, 21, 31, 39, 159; in Didier Eribon's France, 104–10; Golden Age for Western middle class, 33–4, 43; Hillaryland in USA, 87–8; 'meritocracy', 43, 44–6; mobility as vanishing in West, 43–6; move rightwards of blue-collar whites, 95–9, 102, 108–10, 189–91, 194–5; poor whites in USA, 95–6, 112–13; populism in late nineteenth century, 110–11; and post-war centre-left politics, 89–92, 99; 'precariat' ('left-behinds'), 12, 13, 43–8, 50, 91, 98–9, 110, 111, 131; and Trump's agenda, 111, 151, 169, 190; urban liberal elites, 47, 49–51, 71, 87–9, 91–5, 110, 204; West's middle-income problem, 13, 31–2, 34–41
Clausewitz, Carl von, 161
Clinton, Bill, 26, 71, 73, 90, 97–8, 157–9
Clinton, Hillary, 15, 16, 47, 67, 79, 160, 188; 2016 election campaign, 87–8, 91–4, 95–6, 119, 133; reasons for defeat of, 94–5, 96–8
Cold War: end of, 3–5, 6, 7, 74, 77, 78, 117, 121; nuclear near misses, 174; in US popular imagination, 163; and Western democracy, 115–16, 117, 183
Colombia, 72
colonialism, European, 11, 13, 20, 22–3; anti-colonial movements, 9–10; and Industrial Revolution, 13, 23–5, 55–6
Comey, James, 133
communism, 3–4, 5, 6, 105–8, 115
Confucius Institutes, 84

Congress, US, 133–4
Copenhagen summit (2009), 160
Coughlin, Father, 113
Cowen, Tyler, 40, 50, 57
Crick, Bernard, 138
crime, 47
Crimea, annexation of (2014), 8, 173
Cuba, 165
Cuban Missile Crisis (1962), 165, 174
cyber warfare, 176–8
Cyborg, 54

D'Alema, Massimo, 90
Daley, Richard, 189
Danish People's Party, 102
Davos Forum, 19–20, 27, 68–71, 72–3, 91, 121
de Blasio, Bill, 49
de Gaulle, Charles, 106, 116
de Tocqueville, Alexis, 38, 112, 126–7
democracy, liberal: as an adaptive organism, 87; and America's Founding Fathers, 9, 112–13, 123, 126, 138; and Arab Spring, 82; Chinese view of US system, 85–6; communism replaces as bête noire, 115; concept of 'the people', 87, 116, 119–20; damaged by responses to 9/11 attacks, 79–81, 86, 140, 165; and Davos elite, 68–71; de Tocqueville on, 126–7; declining faith in, 8–9, 12, 14, 88–9, 98–100, 103–4, 119–23, 202–3; demophobia, 111, 114, 119–23; economic growth as strongest glue, 13, 37, 103, 201–2; efforts to suppress franchise, 104, 123; elite disenchantment with, 121; elite fear of public opinion, 69, 111, 118; failing democracies (since 2000), 12, 82–3, 138–9; and 'folk theory of democracy', 119, 120; Fukuyama's 'End of History', 5, 14, 181; and global trilemma, 72–3; and Great Recession, 83–4; and Hong Kong, 164; idealism of Rousseau and Kant, 126; illiberal democracy concept, 119, 120, 136–7, 138–9, 204; in India, 201; individual

democracy, liberal – *continued*
  rights and liberty, 14, 97, 120; late
  twentieth century democratic
  wave, 77–8, 83; and mass
  distraction, 127, 128–30; need for
  regaining of optimism, 202–3; need
  to abandon deep globalisation,
  73–4; nineteenth-century fear of,
  114–15; and plural society, 139;
  popular will concept, 87, 118,
  119–20, 126, 137–8; post-Cold War
  triumphalism, 5, 6, 71; post-war
  golden era, 33–4, 43, 89, 116, 117;
  post-WW2 European constitutions,
  116; and 'precariat' ('left-behinds'),
  12, 13, 43–8, 50, 91, 98–9, 110, 111,
  131; the rich as losing faith in,
  122–3; Russia's hostility to, 6–8, 79,
  85; space for as shrinking, 72–3;
  technocratic mindset of elites,
  88–9, 92–5, 111; Trump as mortal
  threat to, 97, 104, 111, 126, 133–6,
  138, 139, 161, 169–70, 178–84,
  203–4; and US-led invasion of Iraq
  (2003), 8, 81, 85; Western toolkit
  for, 77–9; *see also* politics in West
Diamond, Larry, 83
digital revolution, 51–5, 59–66, 67–8,
  174; cyber-utopians, 52, 60, 65;
  debate over future impact, 56; and
  education, 197, 198; exponential
  rate of change, 170, 172, 197;
  internet, 34, 35, 127, 128, 129–30,
  131, 163; internet boom (1990s), 34,
  59; and low productivity growth,
  34, 59, 60; as one-sided exchange,
  66–7; and risk-averse/conformist
  mindset, 40
diplomacy and global politics:
  annexation of Crimea (2014), 8,
  173; China's increased prestige,
  19–20, 26–8, 29–30, 35, 83–5, 159;
  declining US/Western hegemony,
  14, 21–2, 26–8, 140–1, 200–1;
  existential challenges in years
  ahead, 174–84; multipolarity
  concept, 6–8, 70; and nation's
  popular imagination, 162–3;

parallels with 1914 period, 155–61;
  and US 'war on terror', 80–1, 140,
  183; US–China relations, 25–6,
  145–6, 157–61, 165; US–China war
  scenario, 145–53, 161; US–Russia
  relations under Obama, 79
Doha Round, 73
drugs and narcotics, 37–8
Drutman, Lee, 68
Dubai, 48
Durkheim, Émile, 37
Duterte, Rodrigo, 136–7, 138

economists, 27
economy, global *see* global economy;
  globalisation, economic; growth,
  economic
Edison, Thomas, 59
education, 42, 44–5, 53, 55, 197, 198
Egypt, 82, 175
electricity, 58, 59
Elephant Chart, 31–3
Enlightenment, 24, 104
entrepreneurialism, decline of in
  West, 39–40
Erdoğan, Recep Tayyip, 137
Eribon, Didier, 104–10, 111
Ethiopia, 82
Europe: 'complacent classes' in, 40;
  decline of established parties,
  89; geopolitical loss, 141; growth
  of inequality in modern era,
  43; identity politics in, 139–40;
  migration crisis, 70, 100, 140,
  180–1; nationalism in, 10–11,
  102, 108–9; nineteenth-century
  diplomacy, 7–8, 155–6, 171–2;
  post-war constitutions in, 116;
  Putin's interference in, 179, 180; as
  turning inwards, 14
European Commission, 118, 120
European Union, 72, 117–19, 139–40,
  179–80, 181, 201; *see also* Brexit

Facebook, 39, 54, 67, 178
fake news, 130, 148, 178–9
Farage, Nigel, 98–9, 100, 184
fascism, 5, 77, 97, 100, 117

Federal Bureau of Investigation (FBI), 131–2, 133
Felt, Mark, 131–2, 134
financial crisis, global (2008), 27, 29, 30, 91; Atlantic recession following, 30, 63–4, 83–4
financial services, 54
Financial Times, 136, 200
Finland, 139
First World War, 115, 154–5
Flake, Jeff, 134
Florida, Richard, 47, 49, 50, 51
Flynn, Michael, 148, 149
Foa, Roberto Stefan, 123
Ford, Henry, 66–7
Foucault, Michel, 107
France, 15, 37, 63, 102, 104–10, 116; 1968 Paris demonstrations, 188; French Revolution, 3
Franco, General Francisco, 77
Franco-German War (1870–1), 155–6
Frank, Robert H., 30, 35–6, 44
Franklin, Benjamin, 204
Freelancer.com, 63
Friedman, Ben, *The Moral Consequences of Economic Growth*, 38
Friedman, Thomas, 74
Frontex (border agency), 181
FSB, 6
Fukuyama, Francis, 12, 83, 101, 139, 193–4; 'The End of History?' (essay), 5, 14, 181

Garten, Jeffrey, *From Silk to Silicon*, 25
Gates, Bob, 177–8
gay marriage issue, 187, 188
gender, 57
General Agreement on Tariffs and Trade (GATT), 72
Genghis Khan, 25
gentrification, creeping, 46, 48, 50–1
Georgia, Rose Revolution (2003), 79
Germany, 15, 42, 43, 57, 78, 115; far-right resurgence in, 139–40; and future of EU, 180; Nazi, 116, 117, 155, 171; post-war constitution, 116; rise of from late nineteenth

century, 156–7; Trump's attitude towards, 179–80; vocational skills education, 197
gig economy, 62–5
Gladiator (film), 128–9
Glass, Ruth, 46
global economy: centre of gravity shifting eastwards, 21–2, 141; change of guard (January 2017), 19–20, 26–7; emerging middle classes, 21, 31, 39, 159; end of Washington Consensus, 29–30; fast-growing non-Western economies, 20–2; Great Convergence, 12, 13, 24, 25–33; Great Divergence, 13, 22–5; Great Recession, 63–4, 83–4, 192, 193; new protectionism, 19–20, 73, 149; 'precariat' ('left-behinds'), 12, 13, 43–8, 50, 91, 98–9, 110, 111, 131; rapid expansion of China, 20–2, 25–8, 157, 159; spread of market economics, 8, 29; West's middle-income problem, 13, 31–2, 34–41; *see also* globalisation, economic; growth, economic
globalisation, economic: China as new guardian of, 19–20, 26–7; Bill Clinton on, 26; in decades preceding WWI, 155; Elephant Chart, 31–3; Friedman's Golden Straitjacket, 74; Jeffrey Garten's history of, 25; and global trilemma, 72–3; and multinational companies, 26–7; need to abandon deep globalisation, 73–4; next wave of, 32; radical impact of, 12–13; and stateless elites, 51, 71; and Summers' responsible nationalism, 71–2; and technology, 55–6, 73, 174
Gongos (government-organised non-governmental organisations), 85
Google, 54, 67
Gordon, Robert, *The Rise and Fall of American Growth*, 57–8, 59–61
Graham, Lindsey, 134

Greece: classical, 4, 10, 25, 137–8, 156, 200; overthrow of military junta, 77

Greenspan, Alan, 71

growth, economic: and bad forecasting, 27; as Bell's 'secular religion', 37; and digital economy, 54–5, 59, 60; Elephant Chart, 31–3; emerging economies as engine of, 21, 30, 31, 32; Golden Age for Western middle class, 33–4, 43; Robert Gordon's thesis, 57–8, 59–61; and levels of trust, 38–9; as liberal democracy's strongest glue, 13, 37, 103, 201–2; out-dated measurement models, 30–1; technological leap forward (from 1870), 58–9; West's middle-income problem, 13, 31–2, 34–41

Hamilton, Alexander, 78

Harvard University, 44–5

healthcare and medicine, 35, 36, 42, 58, 59, 60, 62, 102, 103, 198

Hedges, Chris, *Empire of Illusion*, 125

Hegel, Friedrich, 161–2

Heilbroner, Robert, 10

Hispanics in USA, 94–5

history: 1930s extremism, 116–17; Chinese economy to 1840s, 22–3; Fukuyama's 'end of history', 5, 14, 181; Great Divergence, 13, 22–5; Hobson's prescience over China, 20–1; and inequality, 41–3; and journalists, 15; Keynes' view, 153–5; Magna Carta, 9–10; of modern democracy, 112–17; nineteenth-century protectionism, 78; nineteenth-century European diplomacy, 7–8, 155–6, 171–2; non-Western versions of, 11; Obama on, 190; Peace of Westphalia (1648), 171; populist surge in late-nineteenth-century USA, 110–11; post-war golden era, 33–4, 43; post-war US foreign policy, 183–4; technological leap forward (from 1870), 58–9; theories

of, 10–11, 14, 190; Thucydides trap, 156–7; utopian faith in technology, 127–8; Western thought on China, 158–9, 161–2; 'wrong side of history' language, 187–8, 190, 191–2; Zheng He's naval fleet, 165–6; *see also* Cold War; Industrial Revolution

Hitler, Adolf, 116, 128, 171

Hobbes, Thomas, 104

Hobsbawm, Eric, 5

Hobson, John, 20, 22–3

Hofer, Norbert, 15–16

homosexuality, 106, 107, 109–10

Hong Kong, 163–4

Hourly Nerd, 63

Hu Jintao, 159

Humphrey, Hubert, 189

Hungary, 12, 82, 138–9, 181

Huntington, Samuel, *The Clash of Civilizations*, 181

Huxley, Aldous, *Brave New World*, 128, 129

illiberal democracy concept, 119, 120, 136–7, 138–9, 204

India: caste system, 202; circular view of history, 11; colonial exploitation of, 22, 23, 55–6; democracy in, 201; future importance of, 167, 200–1; and Industrial Revolution, 23–4; internal migration in, 41; as nuclear power, 175; and offshoring, 61–2; pre-Industrial Revolution economy, 22; rapid expansion of, 21, 25, 28, 30, 58, 200, 201–2; Sino-Indian war (1962), 166; as 'young' society, 39, 200

Indonesia, 21

Industrial Revolution, 13, 22, 23–4, 46, 53; non-Western influences on, 24–5; and steam power, 24, 55–6

inequality: decline in post-war golden era, 43; and demophobia, 122–3; forces of equalisation, 41–3; global top 1 per cent, 32–3, 50–1; growth of in modern era, 13, 41, 43–51; in India, 202; in liberal cities, 49–51;

in nineteenth century, 41; and physical segregation, 46–8; urban–hinterland split, 46–51
infant mortality, 58, 59
inflation, 36
Instagram, 54
intelligence agencies, 133–4
intolerance and incivility, 38
Iran, 175, 193, 194
Iraq War (2003), 8, 81, 85, 156
Isis (Islamic State), 178, 181, 182–3
Islam, 24–5; Trump's targeting of Muslims, 135, 181–3, 195–6
Israel, 175

Jackson, Andrew, 113–14, 126, 134
Jacobi, Derek, 128–9
Japan, 78, 167, 175
Jefferson, Thomas, 56, 112, 163
Jobs, Steve, 25
Johnson, Boris, 48, 118–19
Jones, Dan, 9
Jospin, Lionel, 90
journalists, 15, 65
judiciary, US, 134–5

Kant, Immanuel, 126
Kaplan, Fred, *Dark Territory: The Secret History of Cyber War*, 176–8
Kennedy, John F., 146, 165
Kerry, John, 8
Keynes, John Maynard, 153–5, 156
Khan, A.Q., 175
Khan, Sadiq, 49–50
Kissinger, Henry, 14, 162, 166
knowledge economy, 47, 61
Kreider, Tim, 111
Krugman, Paul, 162
Ku Klux Klan, 98, 111

labour markets: and digital revolution, 52–5, 56, 61–8; and disappearing growth, 37; driving jobs, 56–7, 63, 191; gig economy, 62–5; offshoring, 61–2; pressure to postpone retirement, 64; revolution in nature of work, 60–6, 191–3; security industry, 50; status of technical and service jobs, 197–8; and suburban crisis, 46; wage theft, 192; zero hours contracts, 191
Lanier, Jaron, 66, 67
Larkin, Philip, 188
Le Pen, Marine, 15, 102, 108–10
League of Nations, 155
Lee, Spike, 46
Lee Teng-hui, 158
left-wing politics: and automation, 67; decline in salience of class, 89–92, 107, 108–10; elite's divorce from working classes, 87–8, 89–95, 99, 109, 110, 119; in France, 105–10; Hillaryland in USA, 87–8; and 'identity liberalism', 14, 96–8; McGovern–Fraser Commission (1972), 189; move to personal liberation (1960s), 188–9; populist right steals clothes of, 101–3; Third Way, 89–92; urban liberal elites, 47, 49–51, 71, 87–9, 91–5, 110, 204
Lehman Brothers, 30
Li, Eric, 86, 163–4
liberalism, Western: Chinese hostility to, 84–6, 159–60, 162; crisis as real and structural, 15–16; declining belief in 'meritocracy', 44–6; declining hegemony of, 14, 21–2, 26–8, 140–1, 200–1; elites as out of touch, 14, 68–71, 73, 87–8, 91–5, 110, 111, 119, 204; and 'identity liberalism', 14, 96–8; linear view of history, 10–11; Magna Carta as founding myth of, 9–10; majority-white backlash concept, 12, 14, 96, 102, 104; psychology of dashed expectations, 34–41; scepticism as basis of, 10; and Trump's victory, 11–12, 28, 79, 81, 111; 'wrong side of history' language, 187–8, 190, 191–2; *see also* democracy, liberal
Lilla, Mark, 96, 98
Lincoln, Abraham, 146
Lindbergh, Charles, 117
literacy, mass, 43, 59
Lloyd George, David, 42

Locke, John, 104
London, 46, 47, 48, 49–50, 140
Los Angeles, 50

Machiavelli, Niccolò, 133
Magna Carta, 9–10
Mahbubani, Kishore, 162
Mailer, Norman, *Miami and the Siege of Chicago*, 189
Mair, Peter, 88, 89, 118
Mann, Thomas, 203
Mao Zedong, 163, 165
Marconi, Guglielmo, 128
Marcos, Ferdinand, 136
Marshall, John, 134
Marshall Plan, 29
Marxism, 10, 11, 51, 68, 106, 110, 162
Mattis, Jim, 150–1
May, Theresa, 100, 152, 153
McAfee, Andrew, 60
McCain, John, 134
McMahon, Vince and Linda, 124, 125
McMaster, H. R., 149
media: exposure of Nixon, 131–2; fake news, 130, 148, 178–9; falling credibility in US, 130; in Russia, 129–31, 172–3; television, 84, 128, 129, 130
medicine and healthcare, 35, 36, 42, 58, 59, 60, 62, 102, 103, 198
Medvedev, Dimitry, 79
Meiji Restoration in Japan, 78
mercantilism, 78
'meritocracy', 43, 44–6
Merkel, Angela, 15, 180
Mexico, 29, 114
Middle East, 181, 183
Middle East and North Africans (MENAs, US ethnic category), 95
Midland, Michigan, 194–5
migration, 41, 99–100, 196, 198; current crisis, 70, 100, 140, 180–1; and welfare systems, 101, 102
Milanovic, Branko, 31, 32, 33
Mill, John Stuart, 161, 162
Mineta, Norman, 134
Mitterrand, François, 90, 107
Modi, Narendra, 201

Moldova, Grape Revolution (2009), 79
Mongol China, 25
Monroe Doctrine (1823), 164–5
Moore, Barrington, 12
Morozov, Evgeny, *The Net Delusion*, 129
Mounk, Yascha, 68, 123
Müller, Jan-Werner, 90, 118, 139
multinational companies, 26–7, 69–70
multipolarity, 6–8, 70
Musharraf, Pervez, 80
Muslim Brotherhood in Egypt, 82

Napoleonic Wars, 156
Nathan, Andrew, 84
National Endowment for Democracy (NED), 82
National Front in France, 15, 102, 108–10
National Health Service, 102
nationalism: comeback of, 11, 97, 102, 108–9, 170, 174; and end of Cold War, 5; European, 10–11, 102, 108–9; and global trilemma, 72–3; Summers' responsible nationalism, 71–2
Nato alliance, 135, 140, 179
Navarro, Peter, 149, 167, 180
Negroponte, Nicholas, 127
Netherlands, 102
New York, 49–50, 54
New Yorker, 35
Nixon, Richard, 131–2, 134
non-governmental organisations (NGOs), 85
North American Free Trade Agreement, 73
North Korea, 175
nuclear weapons, 5, 167, 174–6
Nuttall, Paul, 90

Obama, Barack: and AIIB, 84; and Arab Spring, 82; Asia pivot policy, 157, 160–1; election of (2008), 97; and financial sector, 193, 199; gay marriage issue, 188; gender identity order (2016), 187–8; on history's long arc, 190; and Islam, 182; and

nuclear weapons, 175–6; trip to China (2009), 159–60; US–Russia relations, 79; and world trade agreements, 73; 'wrong side of history' language, 187–8, 190
Occupy Wall Street, 139
oikophobia, 111–12, 117
Opium Wars, 23
Orbán, Viktor, 138–9, 181
Organization for Economic Cooperation and Development, 29
Orwell, George, 69, 128
Oxford University, 4

Paine, Thomas, 126
Pakistan, 175
Philippines, 61, 136–7, 138, 160, 202
Philosophy, Politics and Economics (PPE), 4
Plato, 137
politics in West: 1968 Democratic Convention, 188–9; decline of established parties, 88–90; declining faith in system, 8–9, 12, 14, 88–9, 98–100, 103–4, 119–23, 202–3; and disappearing growth, 13; falling voter turnout in UK, 99; left embraces personal liberation (1960s), 188–9; and 'meritocracy', 43–6; move rightwards of working classes, 95–9, 102, 108–10, 189–91, 194–5; and national identity, 71–3; privatising of risk since late 1970s, 191–3; responses to digital revolution, 52–4, 56–8, 59–61, 67–8; Third Way, 89–92; urban–hinterland split, 46–51, 119, 120, 130, 135; US political system, 131–6; voter disdain for elites, 14, 98–100, 110, 119
Pomerantsev, Peter, *Nothing Is True and Everything Is Possible*, 79, 130, 140, 172
populist right: 'alt-right' fringe, 97, 104; America First movement, 117; and automation, 67; cultural and economic anxieties, 190–6; Davos's solution, 69, 70–1; in Europe,

139–40; Andrew Jackson's election (1828), 113–14; and migration crisis, 181; as not democratic, 139; racism as not root cause, 97, 98, 100, 195; Republican Party dog whistles, 190; stealing of the left's clothes, 103; 'take back control' as war cry, 190; and war against truth, 79, 86, 127, 128–31, 172–4, 178–9, 195–6; *see also* Putin, Vladimir; Trump, Donald
Portugal, 77
Primakov, Yevgeny, 6
protectionism, 19–20, 73, 78, 149
Putin, Vladimir: 2012 presidential victory, 130; annexation of Crimea (2014), 8, 173; and fall of Soviet Union, 6; interference in Europe, 179, 180; and Islam, 182; mastery of diversion/confusion, 86, 129, 130–1, 137, 172–3; Medvedev succeeds (2008), 79; replaces Yeltsin as president, 78; Trump's admiration for, 7, 129, 135; and Trump's victory, 7, 12, 79; and US 'war on terror', 80; and US–China war scenario, 146–7, 152–3
Putnam, Robert, 38

Quadruple Alliance, 7
Quah, Danny, 21

race and ethnicity: and 2016 US Presidential election, 94, 95, 96–7, 98; and 'identity liberalism', 14, 96–8; majority-white backlash concept, 12, 14, 96, 102, 104; poor whites in USA, 95–6, 112–13; return of racial politics, 102, 103, 104; US classification data, 94–5; and welfare systems, 101, 102
racism, 97, 98, 99, 100–1, 104, 113–14, 195
Reagan, Ronald, 37
Reagan Democrats, 95, 189
Reeves, Richard, 44
Regional Comprehensive Economic Partnership, 167

remote intelligence, 13, 61–2
Renaissance, 24
Reuther, Walter, 66–7
the rich, 32–3, 50–1, 68, 197; Aristotle
  on, 200; loss of faith in democracy,
  122–3; and rising inequality, 32–3,
  43, 46; Trump's support for, 193,
  195, 196, 199–200
robot economy, 34, 51–5, 56, 60–2, 123
Rodrik, Dani, 72, 73
Rome, classical, 25, 128–9
Roosevelt, Eleanor, 10
Roosevelt, Franklin Delano, 128
Rousseau, Jean-Jacques, 126
RT (Russian state TV channel), 84, 85
Rubin, Robert, 71
Russia: conference on 'polycentric
  world order' (Moscow, 2016), 5–8;
  dissidents' view of West, 140;
  expulsion of Western NGOs, 85;
  as failed democracy, 12, 78, 79, 82,
  173; and fake news, 178; media in,
  129–31, 172–3; metropolitan elites,
  130; and multipolarity, 6–8; and
  nuclear weapons, 175; privatisation
  fire sale in, 79; reality-TV
  politics in, 79, 86, 129–31, 172–3;
  Revolution (1917), 115; and
  Trump, 7, 12, 79; and Washington
  Consensus, 29, 78–9; see also Putin,
  Vladimir; Soviet Union

Sajadpour, Karim, 193, 194–5
Salazar, António de Oliveira, 77
San Bernardino massacre (2015), 182
San Francisco, 49
Sanders, Bernie, 92, 93
Santayana, George, 10
Saudi Arabia, 175, 182
Scandinavia, 43, 101, 197
Schröder, Gerhard, 90
Schwarzman, Stephen, 199–200
science, 72, 171, 172
Scopes Monkey trial, 111
Scruton, Roger, 111–12
Seattle world trade talks (1999), 73
Second World War, 116–17, 163, 169,
  170–1

Sessions, Jeff, 151
Shanghai Cooperation Organization,
  80
Shultz, George, 132
Shultz, Martin, 15
Singapore, 21
Sino-Indian war (1962), 166
slave trade, African, 23, 55, 56
Smith, Adam, The Theory of Moral
  Sentiments, 38–9
Social Darwinism, 162
social insurance systems, 42, 101–3,
  191, 198
social media, 34, 39, 53, 54, 66, 67,
  70, 178
Solow, Robert, 34
South America, 32
South China Sea, 147–8, 160–1
South Korea, 21, 29
Soviet Union, 80, 115, 130, 171, 174;
  collapse of, 6, 78, 168; see also
  Russia
Spain, 43, 63, 77, 140
Stalin, Joseph, 128, 171
suburban crisis, 46–8
Summers, Lawrence, 71
Sun Tzu, 161
Surkov, Vladislav, 172–3
surveillance technologies, 68
Sweden, 101, 122

Taiwan, 145, 158, 164, 165, 166–7, 168;
  and US 'One China' policy, 145–6,
  158; and US–China war scenario,
  145, 151–3
Taiwan Strait, 152, 158
Task Rabbit, 63
taxation, 110, 198, 199–200
technology: age of electricity, 58–9;
  and globalisation, 55–6; leap
  forward (from 1870), 58–9; steam
  power, 24, 55–6; the telegraph, 127;
  as Trump's friend, 131, 171; and
  utopian leaps of faith, 127–8; see
  also digital revolution
television, 84, 128, 129, 130
tesobono crisis, Mexican (2005), 29
Thailand, 21, 82

Thatcher, Margaret, 189–90
Thiel, Peter, 34, 53
Thompson, E.P., 201
Thoreau, Henry David, 127–8
Thrower, Randolph, 132
Tillerson, Rex, 147–8, 161
Toil Index, 35–6
Trans-Pacific Trade Partnership, 73, 167
transport, 54, 55, 56–7, 58, 61;
    self-driving vehicles, 54, 57, 60, 68
Trump, Donald: admiration for
    Putin, 7, 129, 135; and America
    First movement, 117; autocratic/
    authoritarian nature of, 133, 169,
    171, 178–9; Bannon as Surkov of,
    173; Chinese view of, 85–6, 140;
    confusion as strategic goal, 79,
    86, 127, 128, 130, 131, 173, 178–9,
    195–6; foreign policy, 167–70,
    178–80, 181–4; ignorance of
    how other countries think, 161,
    167–9; inaugural address, 135, 146;
    Andrew Jackson comparisons, 113–
    14; and male voters, 57; as mortal
    threat to democracy, 97, 104, 111,
    126, 133–6, 138, 139, 161, 169–70,
    178–84, 203–4; and Muslim ban,
    135, 181, 182; narcissism of, 170;
    need for new Mark Felt/Deep
    Throat, 136; and nuclear weapons,
    175, 176; offers cure worse than
    the disease, 14, 181; plan to deport
    Mexican immigrants, 114, 135;
    poorly educated as base, 103,
    123; promised border wall, 94–5;
    protectionism of, 19–20, 73, 149;
    and pro wrestling, 124; stealing
    of the left's clothes, 101, 103;
    stoking of racism by, 97; support for
    plutocracy, 193, 195, 196, 199–200;
    and Taiwan, 145, 166–7, 168;
    targeting of Muslims, 135, 181–3,
    195–6; and Twitter, 70, 146; and
    UFC, 126; urban–hinterland split
    in 2016 vote, 47–8, 119, 120, 130,
    135; and US political system, 131,
    133–5; US–China war scenario,
    145–53, 161; victory in US

presidential election, 5, 6–7, 11–12,
    15, 28, 47–8, 79, 87, 96–8, 111, 120,
    194–5
Trump: The Game (board game), 7
Tsai Ing-Wen, 151
Tunisia, 12, 82
Turkey, 12, 82, 137, 140, 175
Twitter, 34, 53, 70, 146

Uber, 63
UFC (Ultimate Fighting
    Championship), 125–6, 127
UK Independence Party (UKIP), 90,
    98, 100, 101–2, 190; xenophobia
    during Brexit campaign, 100–1
Ukraine: Orange Revolution (2004),
    79; Putin's annexation of Crimea
    (2014), 8, 173
United States of America (USA):
    1968 Democratic Convention,
    188–9; 2016 presidential election,
    5, 6–7, 11–12, 15, 28, 47–8, 79,
    87–8, 91–8, 119, 130, 133, 135;
    9/11 terrorist attacks, 79–80, 81,
    182; America First movement,
    117; civil rights victories (1960s),
    190; 'complacent classes' in, 40;
    Constitution, 112–13, 163; and
    containment of China, 25–6,
    145–6, 157–61, 165; decline of
    established parties, 89; declining
    hegemony of, 14, 21–2, 26–8,
    140–1, 200–1; domestic terrorist
    attacks, 182, 183; elite–heartland
    divide, 47–8, 119, 130, 135;
    foreign policy since WW2, 183–4;
    gig economy, 63–5; gilded age,
    42–3; growth after 2008 crisis,
    30–1; growth of inequality in
    modern era, 43, 44–8, 49, 50–1;
    history in popular imagination,
    163; Lend-Lease aid to Britain,
    169; middle-income problem in,
    35–41; Monroe Doctrine (1823),
    164–5; murder rate in suburbs,
    47; nineteenth-century migration
    to, 41; Operation Iraqi Freedom,
    8, 81, 85, 156; opioid-heroin

United States of America (USA) –
continued
epidemic, 37–8; Patriot Act, 80;
political system, 112–13, 131–6,
163; post-Cold War triumphalism,
6, 71; primacy in Asia Pacific, 26,
157, 160–1; racial/ethnic make-up
of, 94–6; relations with Soviet
Union *see* Cold War; relative
decline of, 170; 'reverse white flight'
in, 46; technological leap forward
(from 1870), 58–9; vanishing class
mobility in, 43–6; 'war on terror',
80–1, 140, 183; Washington's 'deep
state', 133–4
Universal Basic Income (UBI)
proposals, 196–7
Universal Declaration of Human
Rights, 8–9, 10

Vance, J.D., 108
Venezuela, 82
Versailles Conference (1919), 154
Vienna, Congress of (1814–15), 7
Vietnam, 166

Wallace, George, 113
Walters, Johnnie M., 132
'war on terror', US, 80–1, 140, 183
Warsh, Kevin, 150
Washington Consensus, 29–30, 71, 77,
78–9, 158–9
Washington Post, 132
Weber, Max, 162
welfare systems, 42, 101–3, 191, 198

Western thought: on China, 158–9,
161–2; conceit of primacy of, 4–5,
8–9, 85, 158–9, 162; declining
influence of, 200–1; idea of
progress, 4, 8, 11–12, 37; modernity
concept, 24, 162; non-Western
influences on, 24–5; *see also*
democracy, liberal; liberalism,
Western
WhatsApp, 54
White, Hugh, 25, 158
Wilders, Geert, 102
Wilentz, Sean, 114
Williamson, John, 29
Wilson, Woodrow, 115
Woodward, Bob, 132
Wordsworth, William, 3
World Bank, 84
World Trade Organization (WTO),
26, 72, 149, 150
Wright, Thomas, 180
WWE (World Wrestling
Entertainment), 124–5

Xi Jinping, 19–20, 26, 27, 146, 149,
168, 170; and US–China war
scenario, 150, 152

Yellen, Janet, 150
Yeltsin, Boris, 78, 79
Young, Michael, 45–6
YouTube, 54

Zakaria, Fareed, 13, 119